Crave Bakery:
Gluten Free Cookbook

Crave Bakery: Gluten Free Cookbook

Over 60 Gluten and Dairy Free Recipes
from San Francisco's First
Gluten Free Bakery

10th Anniversary Cookbook

Cameo Edwards

Photography by
New Image Studio
Alexander Warnow
Annabelle Breakey

Crave Bakery
San Francisco

ISBN 978-0-9894239-3-9 (print)

Book layout and formatting by BOOKOW.COM

For S, Lulu and Hugo.

Acknowledgments

I feel like this is my 'Oscar Speech' moment! I've always wanted to publicly give thanks. What better place to thank people than Crave's book of recipes? There are so many people who have made this bakery possible through the years- way too many to list here. But the following people continue to see me through the process to this day.

My mom, for being my cooking and baking inspiration. She effortlessly concocted complicated dishes over the years that I'm still not brave enough to attempt.

My dad, for encouraging my entrepreneurial spirit, talking through many business challenges and all his amazing product photography over the years.

My stepmom, for being an incredible listener and inspiring me with her complex culinary endeavors.

My younger sister, for working her hands in the bakery in the early years, beautiful Crave photography and video creations, and being my constant cheerleader.

My youngest sister and stepdad, for always encouraging me and staying eternally positive about my endeavor.

My dearest friends, Q & J, for being my emotional, marketing and legal support through the years.

My grandparents, who gave me so much including their entrepreneurial spirits.

My business partner, who believed in me, my recipes, the Crave brand and tirelessly strategized on our business plans.

Crave's cake designers, Allison Hobson and Kelly Zubal, who created four years of beautiful cakes for our clients.

My advisor, J, who was a great sounding board and always available with years of food industry, legal and strategy advice.

My colleague and friend, Tina Turbin, who inspired and encouraged me to write this book.

My dogs, Lulu and Hugo, who make me smile all the time and constantly remind me that life shouldn't be so serious.

And S, who is not only one of the smartest, most entrepreneurial and scrappy people I know, he's also my humor-filled, positive light every day.

Endorsements

"Considering how many people with gluten issues also have dairy issues, it has always surprised me that most gluten-free baked goods contain a lot of dairy. Crave Bakery was one of the first gluten-free bakeries to offer dairy-free baked goods that tasted like they were full of butter! Their pretty little Lemon Tarts are corn-free too. Thank you, Crave, for saving tea time!"

Kelly Courson
Creator and Writer at Celiac Chicks
www.celiacchicks.com

"With this cookbook, Cameo has done us a tremendous service. She's taken a decade's worth of trial and error with gluten-free baking and presented us with incredible, easy to follow, "crave-worthy" desserts. There are always special occasions that require a yummy dessert and now you'll know exactly how to achieve fantastic results, even for those not avoiding gluten and dairy! Enjoy!"

Dr. Vikki Petersen, DC, CCN
Founder of HealthNOW Medical Center
Author of "The Gluten Effect"
The Gluten Doctors Blog
www.healthnowmedical.com

"Cameo is amazing for putting so much goodness into one place! So many bakeries guard their "secret" ingredients, but she has made every amazing recipe from Crave Bakery accessible in this deliciously tempting book.

I knew this cookbook would be love at first bite when it started with the legendary Mama Z's Chocolate Cake. But why stop with cake? From Frangipane Tarts to Monster Cookies – there is a reason this collection of bakery recipes is called Crave. I've heard it so many times, 'You'll never believe it's gluten-free and dairy-free.' With Crave I finally agree. The recipes for tender cupcakes, chewy cookies, and flaky tarts will easily make my husband forget that he is gluten-free."

Alisa Fleming
Founder and Chief Editor at Go Dairy Free
www.godairyfree.org

"I met Cameo back when gluten-free was still uncharted territory. I had been diagnosed with celiac disease and she had discovered her own gluten sensitivity, so we connected on a personal level. The gluten-free products on the market left much to be desired in terms of quality and taste, but Cameo had created these delicious treats that made me feel as though I wasn't being deprived one bit!

She was one of the first to recognize the need for dairy-free in addition to gluten-free, and she cared about the ingredients she put into her recipes. I can't say how many times I grabbed a Monster Cookie (my favorite), but I can say that I didn't share them with anyone!"

Alison St. Sure
Founder and Blogger at Sure Foods Living
www.surefoodsliving.com

"Following a gluten-free diet can be difficult, but Crave Bakery makes it a little bit easier by creating some childhood favorites that won't make you feel like you are settling. Their brownies and cookies are sure to please even the pickiest palates. Jon, my son, is extremely picky and he fell in love with the Monster Cookies - a blondie-type, brownie-like cookie with chocolate chunks. The Brownies are dense and fudgy with no telltale sign of the product being gluten-free."

Kimberly Bouldin
Owner and Blogger at Gluten Free Is Life
www.glutenfreeislife.com

Contents

Foreword

I was an avid gluten-free researcher, writer, tester and gluten-free food and company reviewer, known for my diligent work in the gluten-free arena as a celiac advocate up until just about a year ago. I have spread my wings into a few other areas to help all celiacs and those with gluten issues. My original research and reference website www.GlutenFreeHelp.info was voted #2 "by the people" in 2009, which was taken over by my daughter, Miranda Jade Turbin- also celiac.

I spent years being misdiagnosed and once this was resolved there was no looking back. But looking forward meant a major lifestyle change and quickly. Along with this diagnosis came my sincere interest in promoting only the highest quality gluten-free foods of all kinds and businesses with integrity, which came hand-and-glove with honest and dependable people. This led me to an introduction to Cameo Edwards the founder, head baker, and recipe developer for Crave, a San Francisco-based bakery and a thriving company.

The exact moment stands out in my mind to this very day when we were taste-testing Crave's baked goods in my East Coast kitchen. First, my staff and I saw the beautiful presentation in her minimal packaging, and then I bit into my first vanilla cupcake with this killer frosting, next I bit into a chocolate cupcake with yet another amazing frosting, then tasted some wild, incredibly rich and moist brownies, then came these three outstanding tarts. One after the next the flavors were delicious, moist, actually held together like any gluten-loaded counterpart and more important, tasted EXACTLY like those baked goods I had been longing for since being diagnosed. I looked across at my testers and saw the same look on their faces. I will never forget that afternoon!

Then, we had to call her across the country informing her how enamored we were about Crave's baked goods. I thought she'd think we were a bit crazy, yet our excitement was absolutely true. It was a pleasure to deal with a woman and company with such integrity. She informed me that it was not just her recipes but also her select local ingredients, which were part of our experience. Cameo is a woman who truly cared about the health of all celiacs!

We had not taste-tested anything that fresh and delicious. I went on to not only write an extremely positive and broadly published review but produced a 4 minute video review with hopes to help spread the word about Cameo and Crave even more.

Cameo's products are hands-down the best gluten-free baked goods I have ever tasted. I must add, not one of us ever felt a sugar load or ill effects after tasting all her goods.

This is really saying something as we had years of testing, many hours and days in a row. Cameo and I reunited early in 2013. She informed me she had evolved with Crave and now desired to share these incredible proprietary recipes with the world at large commemorating Crave's 10th Anniversary! I was honored when she asked if I'd be part of this revelation, and contribute an introduction to her cookbook. I was and am honored.

It is an absolute pleasure to let you know we really do have Cameo's personal legacy, which comprises Crave's ever popular gluten-free recipes, at OUR finger tips here in this very book. We can all create any Crave gluten-free baked goods, right now in our very own kitchen. This is unbelievable!

Thank you Cameo! You have a heart of gold.

In Good Health,
Tina Turbin

About Tina Turbin

Tina Turbin focuses her efforts as a celiac advocate, researching and writing about the Paleo Diet (inherently gluten-free and grain-free), as well as focusing on Paleo gluten-free recipe developing. Tina is an award winning Paleo gluten-free recipe developer at www.PaleoGlutenFreeRecipes.com, author of the well known and multi-award winning children's titles, Danny the Dragon. Tina is the founder of www.GlutenFreeHelp.info, voted #2 in the world in 2009; turning it over in 2012 to her celiac daughter, Miranda Jade Turbin. Tina is a diagnosed celiac after years of misdiagnosing.

www.TinaTurbin.com
www.PaleoGlutenFreeRecipes.com

History of Crave

Welcome to 10 years of perfected recipes for Crave Bakery. When I opened Crave in 2003, it was the first gluten-free bakery in the San Francisco Bay Area. It was the perfect place, and time, to start an "alternative food" business. This book is a collection of over 60 recipes made in Crave Bakery for our line of high-end grocery desserts or our decadent wedding and party cakes in the Bay Area. I even created a few extras specifically for this book. I am really proud that these recipes have withstood the test of time. Not only are they simple to make, their taste will fool your wheat and dairy-loving friends. On our 10th Anniversary, we have decided to share all our recipes with you.

I have read many, many accounts of others going gluten-free over the years and I know my story is a familiar one. In 2001, I became very sick to my stomach for about a year and half. At first, I thought it was the stress of my job – I worked for a very busy start-up ad agency in downtown San Francisco. After daily and nightly pain and discomfort, I finally gave in to seeing doctors. I first attempted the traditional route and saw a couple different gastroenterologists. They suggested a variety of pharmaceuticals to cure my symptoms. The one that stands out most vividly in my mind was some purple pill that my doctor warned me, "might make me a little tired". This was a definite understatement considering my boyfriend at the time found me on my kitchen floor, so catatonic I was unable to crawl 15 feet to my bed. Another doctor was unable to determine a definitive ailment, and finally diagnosed me with IBS. What was IBS? He couldn't exactly tell me – except that, essentially, I had a "finicky stomach". "But what causes it?", I wanted to know. "How can I fix it? I can't just go on like this. I'm in pain and discomfort ALL THE TIME".

He sent me away without any other suggestions, leaving me frustrated, disappointed and somewhat hopeless. In an effort to give myself the space to sort out my health, I reduced my work schedule to part-time. I remained frustrated with Western Medicine and eventually sought the help of a holistic practitioner. I found Dr. Victoria Hamman in San Francisco. We tried several things together, the Master Cleanse (many of us have done this one!), homeopathy, the Candida Diet, blood tests and allergy tests. Nothing helped, in fact some of these trials even made things worse, temporarily.

Several months of these trials passed and I began preparing for a two-month trip to Thailand that I had scheduled earlier in the year. As the date approached and I quit my job, I realized, I might not be able to travel. I had lost a lot of weight as a result of these various diet and supplement experiments. I had very little energy. In fact, when I went home for Christmas I remember my mom's facial expression, her eyes welling up with tears at how frail I had become. But something in me told me to go Thailand anyway.

I figured, if I can't handle it, I'll just come home. However, after less than a week of eating Thai food, I felt like a miracle had happened. Still, at this point, I had no idea why I had previously felt so bad, but all I cared about was feeling great for the first time in years and I never wanted to leave Thailand! I thought to myself that it must have been the stress and I'm never going back to advertising! And the fact is, I never did go back to advertising. The other fact is that when I came back to the States, I got sick again which was a massive disappointment.

At that point, I began an elimination diet with Dr. Hamman that would last several months. I felt better off wheat but still not great. She suggested that it might actually be gluten. Gluten? What the heck was that?

Of course, I went out and bought everything gluten-free that I could find on the market. And, of course, I felt fantastic. A huge weight was lifted off me. Huge! I finally had a solution. I felt so happy and... normal.

[As a side note, for a long time I didn't know if I had Celiac Disease. I only thought about getting tested after several years on a gluten-free diet. At that point, I was told I would need to eat gluten in full force so I could get an accurate biopsy. My blood tests had come back negative for antibodies. After a few weeks of eating gluten again and feeling absolutely destroyed, I gave up and went back to being gluten-free. I decided knowing that I needed to eat gluten-free was enough for me. I couldn't put my body through that again. These days, I call myself gluten sensitive, which is a grey area that has gotten a lot more attention recently. Dr. Vikki Petersen, who endorsed this cookbook, has focused much of her research on this increasingly common dietary challenge.]

But, despite the relief of this gluten-free discovery, everything I bought tasted like space food (and could practically last as long on the shelf). I couldn't find anything that didn't have a horrible taste, texture and ingredient quality. So, even though I felt physically good, over the next few months I became very frustrated – and then very determined. Remember, this was 2003 and, at that time, NO ONE knew what gluten-free was. From medical doctors to friends and family to grocery stores, I was constantly talking with people and trying to solve this problem. During this discovery phase, I had been baking for myself because I had been craving all of these goodies that I could no longer eat. My love of baking started with my family at a young age. It seemed natural to attempt my own creations. As a result, I created a gluten-free brownie recipe that I was proud of and had been sharing with friends. And then it dawned on me, "There simply aren't any good, upscale GF desserts in grocery stores. Why not sell it? This is San Francisco, a foodie capital. There must be others like me and I want to turn this life challenge into something amazing!"

And there it was plain as day... CRAVE.

As I started making decisions about the company goals and philosophy I realized it was important to make our products dairy-free too. After researching gluten-free quite a bit, I realized that even though I wasn't effected by dairy, so many GF folks were. Other important elements came into the public discussion too: Soy, Corn, Aluminum, Trans Fats, etc. Autistic children seemed to respond well to a Gluten-Free/Casein-Free Diet too. So, I made the decision to keep each product clean and to accommodate other food allergies as much as possible.

With a box of brownies, a logo design and an ingredient list, I boldly scheduled an appointment with a bakery buyer at Rainbow Grocery – my favorite co-op of all time. And this is how cool Rainbow is - they placed an order even though I only had a recipe, a smile, a big set of cojones (or naivety!) and a lot of passion for gluten-free. Because being gluten-free saved my life and spreading the Crave word saved my life in a lot of ways, too. Supplying good GF desserts to others made me feel a lot better about being gluten challenged. So, with my first order in hand, I was able to go to the next store and say, "Rainbow is going to carry them, you should too!". I found a kitchen, ordered supplies and flew by the seat of my pants. The brownies took off and soon I was asked to make chocolate cake, so I created chocolate cake. Then a pumpkin tart for Thanksgiving and I created that, too. Then cupcakes, and on and on. Because there was such a positive response, it felt like people had been waiting for a high-end gluten-free option for quite some time. The true test was when gluten eaters loved our products or even better, bought Crave products for the ingredient quality and didn't even notice they were gluten-free! Crave really snowballed until, at the height of our production, we were selling in 12 states including the whole west coast and the southwest and mountain regions.

In 2009, after several years of customer requests, we began to offer custom-made party and wedding cakes in the Bay Area. Occasionally, we would even make small cakes to ship across the country. These highly creative and customized projects were a lot of fun and garnered some lovely feedback from clients.

2003 was a really exciting time to start a gluten-free business. I know that Crave and other early pioneers paved the way and set a higher standard for today's gluten-free food. My hope is that everyone, Crave fans, and others just discovering our brand for the first time, will love making these desserts as much as we loved creating them for the last decade.

Enjoy our 10th Anniversary cookbook and stay in touch!

About this Book

What follows are some explanations about what you'll find in our book and how best to use it.

The great thing about these recipes is that a casual baker or a full-fledged bakery can use them. They're precise and tested over years in our own bakery. For the most part, because these recipes were developed for production, it also means that they are fairly simple and efficient. While we like the complicated stuff too, this book keeps the process streamlined for each dessert.

We have split the book into six chapters:

1. Before You Get Started
2. Cakes & Cupcakes
3. Frostings & Fillings
4. Brownies & Cookies
5. Tarts
6. Muffins

We provide all measurements in cups and spoons or grams. Why grams instead of ounces? Because you can get a lot more precise with grams. You can measure very small amounts such as 1/8 teaspoon weights. Baking is a precise practice. The more precise you can be, the better the result. Same goes for Crave recipes, using scaled measurements is the most precise way you can use this book. We have gotten as close as possible to spoons or cups in each formula (if you don't have a scale) but the original recipe is based on weight.

All of our recipes were developed to be Gluten-Free and Dairy-Free. Because we discovered that many people who were gluten intolerant were also dairy sensitive or allergic, we wanted to cover both bases. Most recipes are Soy-Free or can easily be made Soy-Free. Most recipes are also Nut-Free. The one exception to Dairy-Free in this book is the addition of peanut butter chips in a couple of recipe variations. Because (at publishing) it's not possible to find dairy-free, all-natural peanut butter chips (and peanut butter is darn good if you can tolerate peanuts!), we gave you the option to add the chips to just a couple select recipes. The beginning of each recipe provides the allergy statement.

Take a look at the beginning of each recipe to also determine how much time it will take, what tools you will need and how much the recipe yields before you start.

Feel free to add your own upgrades to any of our recipes. For instance, once you have some bases from which to work, you can easily create variations on Vanilla Cake, Pastry, Buttercream, Muffins or Pastry Cream.

We've sprinkled helpful tips throughout the book that are relevant to that specific recipe.

We truly hope you enjoy reading about our bakery, our history and making these recipes for yourself!

Before You Get Started

Take some time to read through this first chapter to help you get started. There is a list of Baking Tips to make your experience easier.

Also, check out the recipes organized by level of difficulty so you know where you feel comfortable starting. Lastly, we recommend ingredients to save you some time in your search.

Baking Tips

Here are tips that we've learned over time to make your baking easier! Some of them are specific to gluten-free and allergy-free baking while others are just general baking and decorating tips. These tips are also sprinkled throughout the book in helpful places.

General Tips

Measuring

If possible, use a scale to measure your ingredients. This will ensure that you get a consistent result every time. When measuring out shortening for instance, there can be air bubbles when packing it into a measuring cup. This can work fine but you will most likely get a slightly different result each time. Using a scale for your ingredients also makes the preparation for your recipes go A LOT faster.

If you use a measuring cup for your shortening or butter substitute, make sure it's at room temperature so you can pack it into the cup well and get an accurate measurement.

Be careful with the salt when scaling up. If you're not sure about keeping the salt proportional in a larger recipe, be conservative. You can always taste the batter and add a little bit more but you can't remove it if it's already too salty.

When I first started Crave, I managed to have a call with the famous Flo Braker who wrote a column called The Baker in the SF Chronicle for over 20 years. She told me, quite unexpectedly, that her #1 tip for starting a baking business was to get myself a Kitchen Calc. This would help me do all sorts of measurement conversions. Flo was completely right; this made baking much easier and more efficient. The calculator also has two timers on it.

There is a difference between your liquid measuring cup and your dry measuring cup. One cup of each is a slightly different weight. If you want to be as precise as possible without using a scale, definitely use the dry and liquid cups as they're intended.

With almost all of our recipes, the prevailing denominator is always the egg. Because you can't easily split an egg, all the recipes are almost always based on one or two eggs to make the formula easier.

Take notes whenever you discover something that works slightly better. You could decide you want less chocolate chips next time, or you may want to bake it a few minutes less, or perhaps you want more lemon flavor. Whatever your preference, make a note for next time so you can create a version suited to your specific taste.

Mixing

Always whisk all your dry ingredients to break up clumps. There's nothing worse than a white clump of baking soda in your chocolatey brownie bite!

Whenever possible, try to have your ingredients at room temperature before starting. If you add a very cold ingredient, you can shock a recipe, resulting in a clumped batter.

Scrape the bowl during mixing. Dry ingredients especially can get stuck to the bottom of the mixing bowl. Give it a good scrape to make sure your mixture will be evenly blended.

Baking

Spray your pans, muffin tins, cake rings or glass dishes before adding your batter. Spray a fine, but even, mist. It's really sad when you pop a cake out of the pan and chunks of it stick to the sides – you're left with a tasty mess!

If you don't have pie weights for baking pastry, try using dried beans, lentils or rice. Pie weights are small, heavy objects used to weigh down your pastry when you pre-bake it (also called blind baking). They prevent the crust from pulling away from the sides and bottom of the pan. Line your pastry with parchment paper or aluminum foil to keep beans and pastry from sticking together. Then place beans on top of the lining.

Make it a habit of rotating your baked goods half way through your bake time. Many ovens, including even those in professional kitchens, bake slightly hotter on one side. Rotate your item half way through to get an even bake.

If you have an oven thermometer, use it! Home ovens often aren't calibrated properly and can give you an unexpected result. If you see that your oven is 375 degrees when you set it to 350, you then know that your oven is running 25 degrees hot. You can compensate for that by setting it 25 degrees lower each time. (And for the more serious bakers, you now know that your oven should be recalibrated.)

Lots of things will change your bake time- altitude, humidity, time of year, increasing or decreasing the batter, convection vs. conventional oven, etc. If you're not sure what type of oven you have, it's most likely conventional if your oven is quiet and you don't hear air circulating. Bake times in this book are based on conventional ovens. The best way to determine the bake time in your environment is to be conservative. Check your baking slightly before the recommended time to ensure you don't over-bake and dry out your goodies. Make notes and get it perfect on your next attempt!

Storing

Some batters, doughs, frostings and fillings can be made in advance. See the notes at the end of every recipe to find out.

Keep your flour refrigerated and sealed if possible. This will ensure that it stays fresh and dry much longer.

Salt keeps best when refrigerated too. Especially if you live in a warm climate, the lack of humidity in the fridge prevents clumping.

Serving

As tempting as it is, don't try to remove papers while your muffin/cupcake is still warm, as the cake will most likely stick to the paper. WAIT, until it's completely cool.

Keep your cake refrigerated until 30 - 60 minutes before you want to serve it. Cakes taste best at room temperature.

When slicing your cakes to serve, heat a knife under a stream of very hot water. Dry the knife which will still be hot. The knife will then easily slide through the cake and give you nice, clean cuts.

Decorating

(More detailed decorating tips in Chapter 3)

Sift your powdered sugar through a fine mesh metal strainer before using it for frosting. This will ensure a smooth finish.

Wait for your cupcakes or cakes to cool completely before you frost. Otherwise, the result will be a melted, runny mess.

When frosting a cake, do a 'crumb layer' first. This is your ugly layer of frosting that no one will see. Then do a final pretty, smooth layer on top of that one.

Wrap and refrigerate your cake rounds. AFTER they are cool, you can cut them with a serrated knife into thinner rounds for layer cakes.

Get creative! Combine an unexpected cake batter with a filling or frosting and make your own interesting combinations.

Dough

When working with dough, rub water OR flour on your hands to keep the dough from sticking to you. Brown rice flour works well for this task.

Always flour your surface before placing dough on it. Brown Rice Flour works well for this task too.

Dough can be made in advance of any recipe and stored in the refrigerator for later use.

Gluten/Allergy Free Tips

When using any type of gum (xanthan, guar, etc.), make sure to mix it in with the dry ingredients first. Whisk all the dry ingredients together to distribute the gum evenly. Gums are so fine that they can puff out when you're mixing so whisk slowly!

Don't be heavy handed with your gums. This is the mistake lots of people make to ensure that gluten-free items hold together. The result will be a gummy, mass produced texture.

Potato Starch and Potato Flour are very different. Potato Flour tastes a lot like potatoes. Potato starch is mild. You will know the difference because the starch is very fine and the flour is more granular.

Try enriched versions of Rice, Almond, Coconut and Soy Milk. They seem to be thicker and give a better result in baking – more like whole milk or cream. We recommend the

Original version of your dairy-free drink because Vanilla will change the flavor. If are corn allergic, check to make sure that the Enriched version is corn-free.

Butter, or another oil which remains solid at room temperature, can usually be substituted for Palm Shortening at a 1:1 ratio. We have tried other dairy-free margarines that work just as well too. If your margarine is salted, you will remove or reduce the salt in the recipe.

If you need a sugar-free recipe, we found that sugar can be substituted quite well with sugar-free Xylitol at a 1:1 ratio.

Try to get grains that are very finely milled if you have the option. The finer the mill, the better the texture and quality of your finished products.

Substituting for Wheat Flour

Say you have an old family recipe (containing gluten) which you want to make Gluten-Free. At Crave, we developed our own combination to substitute for wheat flour which we have detailed in the Ingredients section.

Recipe Levels

If you're just starting out as a baker (or a gluten-free baker), take a look at these recipe categories to determine where to begin. They are arranged by level of difficulty, beginning with the easiest.

Beginner

- ▷ Vanilla Cake
- ▷ Vanilla Cake Variations
- ▷ Spiced Banana Cake
- ▷ Chocolate Frosting
- ▷ Vanilla Frosting
- ▷ Monster Cookie
- ▷ Monster Cookie Variations
- ▷ "Oatmeal" Raisin Cookie
- ▷ "Oatmeal" Raisin Cookie Variations
- ▷ Summer Strawberry Muffins
- ▷ Autumn Pumpkin Muffins
- ▷ Autumn Pumpkin Muffin Variations
- ▷ Muffin Base and Variations
- ▷ Spiced Banana Muffins

Intermediate

- ▷ Mama Z's Chocolate Cake
- ▷ Pink Velvet Cake
- ▷ Chocolate Glaze
- ▷ Pink Velvet Frosting
- ▷ Chocolate Mousse
- ▷ Mocha Mousse
- ▷ Dark Chocolate Brownie
- ▷ Dark Chocolate Brownie Variations
- ▷ Chocolate Muffins

Advanced

- ▷ Swiss Meringue Buttercream
- ▷ Swiss Meringue Buttercream Variations
- ▷ Pink Velvet Buttercream
- ▷ Vanilla Pastry Cream
- ▷ Pastry Cream Variations
- ▷ Pumpkin Tart
- ▷ Lemon Tart
- ▷ Apple Frangipane Tart
- ▷ Apricot Frangipane Tart
- ▷ Fresh Fruit Tart

Ingredients

Following is a list of ingredients (and their descriptions) from the recipes in this book. We have made suggestions about our favorite, high quality brands because these manufacturers have clearly stated Gluten-Free in their product descriptions or company info.

Disclaimer: We still recommend checking with the manufacturer first and reading ingredient labels to be sure that this information is up to date. At publishing, this is the most current info. But manufacturers do periodically change ingredients to suit their needs. Hopefully, this list saves you a little work.

Flours/Starches

▷ Tapioca Flour is a grain-free starch, native to Brazil, derived from cassava root. Our favorite is from Bob's Red Mill.

▷ Potato Starch is starch extracted from potatoes and used as a thickener. Our favorite is from Bob's Red Mill.

▷ Brown Rice Flour is a mild tasting flour that has been ground from unmilled rice grains. Our favorites are from Bob's Red Mill and Authentic Foods.

▷ Sweet Rice Flour (can be white-milled or brown-unmilled) is different than white or brown rice flour which cannot be substituted for Sweet Rice Flour. Sweet Rice Flour is used in Asian cooking and is also known as 'sticky rice' or 'glutinous rice'. This ingredient is one of the keys to light, fluffy and smooth recipes. Sweet Rice Flour is finely milled and has a light texture. Both Bob's Red Mill and Authentic Foods make great quality versions.

▷ Flax Seeds or Flax Meal: You can either buy ground flax meal or whole flax seeds and grind them yourself in your coffee grinder, and you can get both from Bob's Red Mill: Bob's Red Mill Flax Seeds and Bob's Red Mill Flax Meal.

▷ Almond Meal is ground almonds. Almond Flour comes from blanched, ground almonds and is finer than Almond Meal. But sometimes these names are used interchangeably (as Bob's Red Mill does). For the recipes in this book, the less finely milled Almond Meal works the best. Our favorite is from Bob's Red Mill.

Oils

▷ Palm Shortening is a non-hydrogenated and cholesterol-free oil that is solid at room temperature. It works just like butter in recipes. We like Spectrum because they are a responsible grower.

▷ High Heat Canola Spray is great for baking. It won't burn and it has a very mild flavor. Spectrum makes our favorite.

Milk Alternatives

▷ Soy Milk or Rice Milk (or your non-dairy preference) are used in this book. Try the Original/Enriched style for maximum creaminess. (Note that we've found Enriched versions may contain corn.) Even though Vanilla probably tastes better on your cereal, it will change the taste of the recipe, so use Original flavor instead. Our recipes work best with their recommended non-dairy option. However, you can try substituting any other dairy-free milk you prefer. A few that we like include:
▷ Rice Dream Original (corn-free)
▷ Rice Dream Organic Original Enriched (may contain corn)
▷ Pacific Soy Milk Original (corn-free)

Baking Aids

▷ Our favorite Baking Soda is Bob's Red Mill Baking Soda.
▷ Our preferred Gluten-Free, Aluminum-Free, Corn-Free Baking Powder is Hain's Featherweight Baking Powder.
▷ Xanthan Gum helps to replace gluten's stickiness. If you have a corn allergy, make sure your xanthan gum is corn-free such as the one from Bob's Red Mill.
▷ We prefer Sea Salt for its purity. If you are using salt in frosting, it's best to use a fine grained version such as Selina Naturally Fine Ground Celtic to make sure you don't get a large salty chunk.

Sugar

For sugar, it's up to you whether you choose refined or unrefined sugar. Most sugars are gluten-free but check with the manufacturer to make sure. Finer grained sugars work better in frostings. Sucanat and Turbinado are coarse grained sugars.

Powdered Sugar very often has cornstarch in it. We like Organic Wholesome Sweeteners. Although, you must read the label because some of their powdered sugar contains tapioca flour and some contains cornstarch. We recommend their Organic Powdered Sugar, Organic Sucanat, and Organic Sugar.

Xylitol is a natural sweetener, can be substituted 1:1 for sugar and works well for diabetics. NOW Foods Xylitol is derived from non-GMO corn.

Decorating

We recommend using All-Natural Food Coloring, but be aware that natural colors will always be more pale in comparison to conventional food coloring. You won't get those same vibrant colors but you can still make some really pretty pastels.

 ▷ For All-Natural Sugar Sprinkles we recommend Maggie's Naturals
 ▷ For more experienced decorators who want to use Fondant, Vanilla Satin Ice is our favorite.
 ▷ Conventional, Gluten-Free Food Coloring. Wilton's are not all-natural but are gluten-free. We recommend the Wilton Icing Colors.

Spices

Some of our favorite spices include:

 ▷ Spicely Organic Cinnamon
 ▷ Spicely Organic Allspice
 ▷ Spicely Organic Nutmeg
 ▷ Spicely Organic Cardamom

Extracts

We recommend the following extracts:

 ▷ Lemon Extract from either Spicely or Nielsen Massey
 ▷ Orange Extract from either Spicely or Nielsen Massey
 ▷ Madagascar Pure Vanilla from Nielsen Massey
 ▷ Lavender Extract from Silver Cloud
 ▷ Almond Extract from Nielsen Massey

Chocolate

There are several great chocolates that we use:

 ▷ Sunspire Organic Semi-Sweet Chocolate Chips*
 ▷ Sunspire Organic Bittersweet Chocolate Chips*
 ▷ Scharffen Berger Unsweetened Baking Chocolate
 ▷ Scharffen Berger Unsweetened Cocoa Powder
 ▷ Scharffen Berger Bittersweet Chocolate*

▷ Sunspire Non-Hydrogenated Peanut Butter Chips (only if you can tolerate soy, dairy and peanuts)

*Note- if you have a Soy-Allergy, Bittersweet (also known as Dark Chocolate) and Semi-Sweet Chocolates usually have soy lecithin. Unsweetened Baking Chocolate does not, so look for the recipes in this book that have Unsweetened Baking Chocolate or Cocoa instead.

Preserves

▷ Apricot Preserves from Bonne Maman
▷ Raspberry Preserves from Bonne Maman

Eggs

We recommend your local Free-Range Eggs. Whenever possible, make an animal conscious choice.

Wheat Flour Substitute

If you have an old family recipe into which you want to substitute Gluten-Free flour instead, these proportions make approximately one cup of really nice GF Flour. You can double or triple this recipe and save some in the refrigerator for later use. If you make extra, make sure you combine it really well to get the xanthan gum and all flour evenly distributed throughout the mix. A shaken jar works the best.

Our wheat flour substitute blend:

- ▷ 1/2 cup Sweet Rice Flour (79.4 g)
- ▷ 1/3 cup + 2 tsp. Potato Starch (68 g)
- ▷ 1/4 cup Tapioca Flour (14.2 g)
- ▷ 1/2 tsp. Xanthan Gum (1 g)

Cakes and Cupcakes

As the cupcake craze rages on, here are our favorite cake recipes, great for both large cakes and cupcakes. We worked hard to create fluffy, non-grainy, moist textures in all the cake bases.

Combine them with the frosting or filling of your choice in the next chapter for your perfect dessert.

Mama Z's Chocolate Cake

Gluten-Free, Dairy-Free, Soy-Free, Nut-Free, Corn-Free

Mama Z's Chocolate Cake is named after my mom. When first testing this product, we did a Pepsi style challenge (think 80's!) with several chefs at high-end San Francisco restaurants. And guess what? They couldn't detect any ingredient substitutions. This is the most moist and chocolatey GF cake I've had. I really, really love the texture and flavor of this recipe.

Mama Z's Chocolate Cake Recipe

Gluten-Free, Dairy-Free, Soy-Free, Nut-Free, Corn-Free

Prep Time: 25 min, Bake Time: 25 min

Makes: 1052 g - Enough for One 8″ Round, Two 6″ Rounds, Five 4″ Rounds or 12 Cupcakes

Note: If you want to make a four layer 8″ cake, double this recipe. Bake two 8″ rounds and when cool, slice them lengthwise to make four layers total.

Note: This recipe is Corn-Free as long as your Apple Sauce has no high fructose corn syrup.

Tools

- ✓ Mixer or Beaters
- ✓ Whip Attachment
- ✓ Medium Pot
- ✓ Three Bowls
- ✓ Rubber Spatula
- ✓ Whisk
- ✓ Dry Measuring Cups
- ✓ Liquid Measuring Cup
- ✓ Measuring Spoons
- ✓ Cake or Muffin Pans
- ✓ Cupcake Papers if you make Cupcakes
- ✓ Scale if you have one (for measuring by weight)

Ingredients

- ✓ 1/2 cup Unsweetened Baking Chocolate (85 g)
- ✓ 1/2 cup Palm Shortening (94 g)
- ✓ 1 cup + 1 Tbsp. Sugar (216 g)
- ✓ 2 Eggs (99 g)
- ✓ 1/2 cup Applesauce (130 g)
- ✓ 1/2 cup Sweet Rice Flour (79 g)
- ✓ 2 Tbsp. Tapioca Flour (14 g)
- ✓ 1/3 cup + 2 tsp. Potato Starch (68 g)
- ✓ 1/3 cup Cocoa (28 g)
- ✓ 1 tsp. Baking Soda (5.3 g)
- ✓ 1/2 tsp. Salt (2.5 g)
- ✓ 1 tsp. Baking Powder (2.7 g)

- ✓ 1/2 tsp. Xanthan Gum (1 g)
- ✓ 1 cup Water (227 g)
- ✓ Gluten-Free Baking Spray

Let's Get Baking

1 Preheat oven to 350 degrees.

2 Melt Unsweetened Baking Chocolate and Shortening over a double boiler. While Chocolate and Shortening are melting, combine all dry ingredients in a medium bowl. Whisk these ingredients to break up any lumps: Sweet Rice Flour, Tapioca Flour, Potato Starch, Cocoa, Baking Soda, Salt, Baking Powder, Xanthan Gum.

3 Once the Chocolate and Shortening are runny, pour into the mixer. Add Sugar to the mixer. Using the whip attachment, mix on medium speed until sugar is completely melted.

4 Add Eggs, mix on medium just until combined. Then add Applesauce, mix on medium just until combined.

5 Scrape the bottom of the bowl with the rubber spatula if needed and mix again until blended.

6 Add dry ingredients and water, half at a time and mix on low to reduce splashing. Give the bowl one final scrape and then mix on high for 20 seconds or so to fully combine.

7 Spray your cake rings, muffin pans, cake pans or line your muffin pans with papers.
   - ▷ If you're using an 8″ cake pan, use all of the cake batter.
   - ▷ If you're using 6″ cake pans, use 526 g of cake batter per pan. (Or about half the batter)
   - ▷ If you're using 4″ cake rings, use 210 g of cake batter per ring. (Or about 1/5 batter)
   - ▷ For cupcakes use approximately 87 g of batter per cupcake. (Or about 12 Cupcakes)

8 Bake for 12 minutes, rotate and bake for another 13 minutes or until tester comes out clean. For larger cakes you may need to bake an additional 5 minutes. Cake should be pulling away from edges of pan slightly.

Tip: This batter can be refrigerated for later use. It will separate but you can stir it up until it's blended again and bake it the next day if necessary.

Favorite Combinations

- ▷ Tuxedo DreamCups filled with Swiss Meringue Buttercream
- ▷ Layer Cake filled with Mocha Mousse and finished with Chocolate Glaze (the original frosting on the Mama Z's cake sold in stores)
- ▷ Layer cake filled with Vanilla Pastry Cream and frosted with Vanilla Frosting
- ▷ Layer cake filled with Chocolate Mousse and frosted with Chocolate Lavender Buttercream

Vanilla Cake

Gluten-Free, Dairy-Free, Soy-Free, Nut-Free, Corn-Free

Wow, did I miss white and yellow cake when I went gluten-free. That fluffy, light, spongy, moist cake! This recipe was one of the holy grails of gluten-free baking for me and it took more iterations than I care to admit to finally get it just right. With this recipe you can make cakes, frosted or filled cupcakes, minis... pretty much any size. It's stable enough to make larger layer cakes too.

Vanilla Cake Recipe

Gluten-Free, Dairy-Free, Soy-Free, Nut-Free, Corn-Free

Prep Time: 20 min, Bake Time: 20 min

Makes: 801 g, Enough for One 8″ Round, Two 6″ Rounds, Four 4″ Rounds or 12 Cupcakes

Note: If you want to make a four layer 8″ cake, double this recipe. Bake two 8″ rounds and when cool, slice them lengthwise to make four layers total.

Tools

- ✓ Mixer or Beaters
- ✓ Paddle Attachment
- ✓ Two Bowls
- ✓ Rubber Spatula
- ✓ Whisk
- ✓ Dry Measuring Cups
- ✓ Liquid Measuring Cup
- ✓ Measuring Spoons
- ✓ Cake or Muffin Pans
- ✓ Cupcake Papers if you make Cupcakes
- ✓ Scale if you have one (for measuring by weight)

Ingredients

- ✓ 1/2 cup Palm Shortening (113 g)
- ✓ 1 cup Sugar (210 g)
- ✓ 2 Eggs (99 g)
- ✓ 2 tsp. Vanilla (8 g)
- ✓ 3 Tbsp. Tapioca Flour (20 g)
- ✓ 3/4 cup Sweet Rice Flour (119 g)
- ✓ 1/2 cup + 1 Tbsp. Potato Starch (102 g)
- ✓ 2 tsp. Baking Powder (5.4 g)
- ✓ 1/2 tsp. Baking Soda (2.7 g)
- ✓ 3/4 tsp. Xanthan Gum (1.5 g)
- ✓ 1/4 tsp. Salt (1.3 g)
- ✓ 1/2 cup Rice Milk (119 g) [We recommend Original flavor. Vanilla changes the taste of the batter.]
- ✓ Gluten Free Baking Spray

Let's Get Baking

1 Preheat oven to 350 degrees.

2 Beat Shortening and Sugar for three minutes on high with paddle attachment until fluffy.

3 Scrape bowl, add Egg and Vanilla, and beat another two minutes on high.

4 Whisk together the dry ingredients- Tapioca Flour, Sweet Rice Flour, Potato Starch, Baking Powder, Baking Soda, Xanthan Gum and Salt. Whisk until lumps disappear.

5 Alternate adding the whisked dry ingredients and Rice Milk into the mixer, half of each at a time.
   Tip: Whenever possible, try to have your ingredients at room temperature before starting. If you add a very cold ingredient, you can shock a recipe, resulting in a clumped batter.

6 Beat until smooth and fully combined. About 2 minutes.

7 Spray your cake rings, muffin pans, cake pans or line your muffin pans with papers.

8 Transfer the batter into your pan:
   ▷ If you're using an 8" cake pan, use all of the cake batter.
   ▷ If you're using 6" Cake pans, use 400 g of cake batter per pan. (Or about 1/2 batter)
   ▷ If you're using 4" Cake rings, use 200 g of cake batter per ring. (Or about 1/4 batter)
   ▷ For Cupcakes use approximately 66 g of batter per cupcake or fill each paper about 2/3. (Or about 12 Cupcakes)

9 For cupcakes or smaller cakes, bake for 10 minutes, rotate and bake for another 10 minutes. For larger cakes you may need to bake an additional 5 minutes.

10 Remove from oven when the tester comes out clean.

Tip: Keep your cake refrigerated until 30 - 60 minutes before you want to serve it. Cakes taste best at room temperature.

Favorite Combinations

   ▷ Cherub DreamCups filled with Swiss Meringue Buttercream
   ▷ Layer cake filled with Orange Cream and frosted with Swiss Meringue Buttercream
   ▷ Layer cake filled with Cinnamon Cream and frosted with Dark Chocolate Buttercream
   ▷ Layer cake filled with Vanilla Pastry Cream and frosted with Lemon Buttercream
   ▷ Layer cake filled with Chocolate Mousse and frosted with Chocolate Frosting
   ▷ Layer cake filled with Cardamom Cream and frosted with Vanilla Cardamom Buttercream

Variations on Vanilla Cake

Toasted Coconut Cake

Gluten-Free, Dairy-Free, Soy-Free, Nut-Free, Corn-Free

Prep Time: 22 min, Bake Time: 20 min

A toasty, rich version of the Vanilla Cake that becomes mouth watering when topped with our Dark Chocolate Buttercream.

Additional Ingredients

✓ 1 cup Shredded Coconut (88 g)

Let's Get Baking

1 Spread the coconut on a baking sheet so there is a lot of surface area. Toast the coconut in the toaster or oven briefly. Pay close attention so they don't burn! About 2 - 3 minutes until you can start to smell the coconut.

2 Follow all directions for the Vanilla Cake.

3 After you've finished mixing all dry ingredients and Rice Milk in the Vanilla Cake batter, add the Toasted Coconut pieces to the batter. Fold it all together. Combine it until the coconut is evenly distributed.

4 Follow all baking instructions for the Vanilla Cake.

Favorite Combinations

▷ Cupcakes decorated with Dark Chocolate Buttercream
▷ Layer cake filled with Cardamom Cream and frosted with Vanilla Frosting

Lemon Zest Cake

Gluten-Free, Dairy-Free, Soy-Free, Nut-Free, Corn-Free

Prep Time: 22 min, Bake Time: 20 min

Tangy, light and sweet cake! The zest gives this cake that extra lemony taste.

Additional Ingredients

- ✓ 1/3 cup Fresh Lemon Juice (75 g) [2 - 3 Lemons depending on how juicy they are.]
- ✓ Zest from Two Lemons

Let's Get Baking

1 Zest two lemons.

2 Squeeze the lemons, careful to remove the seeds. You will need 1/3 cup (75 g) of fresh lemon juice.

3 Follow all directions for the Vanilla Cake.

4 After you've finished mixing all dry ingredients and Rice Milk in the Vanilla Cake recipe, add 1/3 cup fresh squeezed Lemon Juice. Finally, add the zest. Fold it all together, and the lemon will make your batter lighter and fluffier. Don't over mix it, just combine it evenly.

5 Follow all baking instructions for the Vanilla Cake.

Favorite Combinations

- ▷ Cupcakes decorated with Lemon Buttercream
- ▷ Layer cake filled with Lemon Cream and Lemon Buttercream

Toasty Pecan Cake

Gluten-Free, Dairy-Free, Soy-Free, Corn-Free

Prep Time: 22 min, Bake Time: 20 min

A nutty, rich cake delicious with our Buttercream.

Additional Ingredients

✓ 3/4 cup of Chopped Pecans (96 g). Don't chop too fine, about 1/4" pieces.

Let's Get Baking

1 Toast the pieces in the toaster or oven briefly. Pay close attention so they don't burn! About 3-4 minutes until you can start to smell them and the nutty aroma is released.

2 Follow all directions for the Vanilla Cake.

3 After you've finished mixing all dry ingredients and Rice Milk in the Vanilla Cake recipe, add the Toasted Pecan pieces to the batter. Fold it all together. Combine it until the nuts are evenly distributed.

4 Follow all baking instructions for the Vanilla Cake.

Tip: Keep your cake refrigerated until 30 - 60 minutes before you want to serve it. Cakes taste best at room temperature.

Favorite Combinations

▷ Cupcakes decorated with Cinnamon Buttercream
▷ Layer cake filled with Vanilla Pastry Cream and frosted with Cinnamon Buttercream

Spiced Banana Cake

Gluten-Free, Dairy-Free, Nut-Free, Soy-Free, Corn-Free

How do you use overly ripe bananas and turn them into something moist, rich and decadent? A Spiced Banana Cake of course. Clients loved this cake combined with Vanilla Pastry Cream, Chocolate Mousse or Swiss Meringue Buttercream. An upscale twist on banana bread.

Spiced Banana Cake Recipe

Gluten-Free, Dairy-Free, Nut-Free, Soy-Free, Corn-Free

Prep Time: 20 min, Bake Time: 20 min

Makes: 691 g, Enough for One 8″ Round, Two 6″ Rounds, Four 4″ Rounds or 12 Cupcakes

Note: If you want to make a four layer 8″ cake, double this recipe. Bake two 8″ rounds and when cool, slice them lengthwise to make four layers total.

Tools

- ✓ Mixer or Beaters
- ✓ Whip Attachment
- ✓ Three Bowls
- ✓ Rubber Spatula
- ✓ Whisk
- ✓ Dry Measuring Cups
- ✓ Measuring Spoons
- ✓ Masher (or Fork)
- ✓ Cake or Muffin Pans
- ✓ Cupcake Papers if you make Cupcakes
- ✓ Coffee Grinder if you need to grind Flax Seeds
- ✓ Scale if you have one (for measuring by weight)

Ingredients

- ✓ 1 cup = approximately 3 medium mashed, very ripe bananas (250 g)
- ✓ 2 Tbsp. Rice Milk (31 g) [We recommend Original flavor. Vanilla changes the taste of the batter.]
- ✓ 1 ½ Tbsp. Tapioca Flour (11 g)
- ✓ 1/2 cup Sweet Rice Flour (79 g)
- ✓ 1/4 cup Potato Starch (51 g)
- ✓ 3/4 tsp. Baking Soda (4 g)
- ✓ 1 tsp. Baking Powder (2.7 g)
- ✓ 1/2 tsp. Cinnamon 2 g
- ✓ 1/4 tsp. Salt (1.3 g)
- ✓ 1/2 Tbsp. Flax Meal (4g) [or if you prefer instead- 1/2 tsp. Xanthan Gum (1 g)]
- ✓ 1/3 cup Palm Shortening (77 g)
- ✓ 3/8 cup Sugar (79 g)
- ✓ 2 Eggs (99 g)

✓ Gluten-Free Baking Spray

Let's Get Baking

1 Preheat oven to 350 degrees.

2 Mash your Bananas. Then mix with the Rice Milk and set aside.

3 If you choose to use Flax Meal instead of Xanthan Gum, grind Flax Seeds if necessary to make the Flax Meal.

4 Whisk together the dry ingredients to remove clumps and set aside: Tapioca Flour, Sweet Rice Flour, Potato Starch, Baking Soda, Baking Powder, Cinnamon, Salt, Flax Meal OR Xanthan Gum.
   Tip: Always whisk all your dry ingredients to break up chunks. There's nothing worse than a white clump of baking soda in your bite of cake!

5 Using the whip attachment of the mixer, cream together the Shortening and Sugar until light and fluffy, about 3 minutes.

6 Add the Eggs, one at a time, beating well after each to incorporate air. Add the Bananas and Rice milk until combined. Add the dry ingredients, half at a time, mixing gently just until blended (this ensures a delicate crumb and prevents the batter from deflating). Scrape the bowl with the rubber spatula and give one final mix until fully combined.

7 Spray your cake rings, muffin pans, cake pans or line your muffin pans with papers.
   ▷ If you're using an 8" Cake pan, use the all cake batter.
   ▷ If you're using 6" Cake pans, use 346 g of cake batter per pan. (Or about half the batter)
   ▷ If you're using 4" Cake rings, use 173 g of cake batter per ring. (Or about 1/4 batter)
   ▷ For cupcakes use approximately 57 g of batter per cupcake. (Or about 12 Cupcakes)

8 For cupcakes, bake for 10 minutes, rotate and bake for another 10 minutes. Remove from oven when tester comes out clean, a few clinging crumbs are OK. For larger cakes you may need to bake an additional 5-10 minutes. Cake should be pulling away from edges of pan slightly.

Favorite Combinations

   ▷ Cupcakes decorated with Chocolate Glaze- as shown in photo
   ▷ Layer cake filled with Chocolate Mousse and Frosted with Dark Chocolate Buttercream, or with Cinnamon Cream and Swiss Meringue Buttercream

Pink Velvet Cake

Gluten-Free, Dairy-Free, Soy-Free, Nut-Free, Corn-Free

We had been asked to create a Red Velvet cake for many years. However, since we avoid artificial colors, ingredients and additives at all costs, Red Velvet just didn't seem to be a realistic option. In 2011, with Breast Cancer Awareness Month approaching, we wanted to do something to honor these women, and I had a brainstorm to make Pink Velvets instead. Just the right amount of cocoa and chocolate resulted in the pinkish hue of the cake. On top we created the Pink Frosting, made from all-natural beet dye. Voila! Pink Velvets instead of Red. These are also great for Valentine's Day, Mother's Day and any old girly day.

Pink Velvet Cake Recipe

Gluten-Free, Dairy-Free, Soy-Free, Nut-Free, Corn-Free

Prep Time: 25 min, Bake Time: 20 min

Makes: 810 g, Enough for One 8″ Round, Two 6″ Rounds, Five 4″ Rounds or 12 Cupcakes

Note: If you want to make a four layer 8″ cake, double this recipe. Bake two 8″ rounds and when cool, slice them lengthwise to make four layers total. This is Corn-Free as long as your Apple Sauce has no high fructose corn syrup.

Tools

- ✓ Mixer or Beaters
- ✓ Medium Pot
- ✓ Four Bowls
- ✓ Rubber Spatula
- ✓ Whisk
- ✓ Dry Measuring Cups
- ✓ Liquid Measuring Cup
- ✓ Measuring Spoons
- ✓ Cake or Muffin Pans
- ✓ Cupcake Papers if you make Cupcakes
- ✓ Scale if you have one (for measuring by weight)

Ingredients

- ✓ 16 g or .6 oz. Unsweetened Baking Chocolate
- ✓ 1/2 cup Palm Shortening (103 g)
- ✓ 1 cup Sugar (199 g)
- ✓ 2 Eggs (99 g)
- ✓ 1 ¼ Tbsp. Applesauce (25 g)
- ✓ 1 ½ tsp. Vanilla Extract (6 g)
- ✓ 2/3 cup Sweet Rice Flour (105 g)
- ✓ 3 Tbsp. Tapioca Flour (18 g)
- ✓ 1/2 cup Potato Starch (90 g)
- ✓ 1 Tbsp. Cocoa (5.3 g)
- ✓ 3/4 tsp. Baking Soda (4 g)
- ✓ 1/4 tsp. Sea Salt (1.3 g)
- ✓ 1 ¾ tsp. Baking Powder (4.7 g)
- ✓ 3/4 tsp. Xanthan Gum (1.5 g)

✓ 1/4 cup Water (43 g)
✓ 1/3 cup Rice Milk (89 g) [We recommend Original flavor. Vanilla changes the taste of the batter.]
✓ Gluten-Free Baking Spray

Let's Get Baking

1 Preheat oven to 350 degrees.

2 Melt Unsweetened Chocolate and Palm Shortening over a double boiler. While Chocolate and Shortening are melting, combine all dry ingredients in a medium bowl. Whisk these ingredients to break up any lumps: Sweet Rice Flour, Tapioca Flour, Potato Starch, Cocoa, Baking Soda, Salt, Baking Powder, Xanthan Gum.

3 Put Water and Rice Milk together in a bowl.

4 Once the Chocolate and Shortening are runny, pour into the mixer. Add Sugar to the mixer. Using the whip attachment, mix on medium speed until sugar is completely melted.

5 Add Eggs, mix on medium just until combined. Then add Applesauce, mix on medium just until combined.

6 Scrape the bottom of the bowl with the rubber spatula if needed and mix again until blended.

7 Add dry ingredients and Water/Rice Milk, half at a time and mix on low to reduce splashing. Give the bowl one final scrape and then mix on high for 20 seconds or so to fully combine.

8 Spray your cake rings, muffin pans, cake pans or line your muffin pans with papers.
   ▷ If you're using an 8" cake pan, use all of the cake batter.
   ▷ If you're using 6" cake pans, use 404 g of cake batter per pan. (Or about half the batter)
   ▷ If you're using 4" cake rings, 161 g of cake batter per ring. (Or about 1/5 batter.)
   ▷ For cupcakes use approximately 67 g of batter per cupcake. (Or about 12 Cupcakes)

   Tip: Spray your cake pans, muffin pans or cake rings before adding your batter. Spray a fine, but even, mist. It's really sad when you pop a cake out of the pan and chunks of it stick to the sides – you're left with a tasty mess!

9 Bake cupcakes for 10 minutes. Rotate. Bake for another 10 minutes or until tester comes out clean. For larger cakes you may need to bake an additional 5 minutes. Cake should be pulling away from edges of pan slightly.

10 Frost with Pink Vanilla Buttercream or Pink Vanilla Frosting.

Frostings and Fillings

We all know that the cake is the foundation but the key to towers of moist cake is layers! Between each layer, sandwich any of these delicious gluten-free and dairy-free fillings. Then smother the outside with your choice of frosting.

All recipes are dairy-free. Feel free to use butter instead of shortening if you prefer.

Frostings

I'm the kind of person who uses crackers as a vehicle for cheese. And sometimes I want my cake to be a vehicle for frosting. We've developed an array of decadent frostings for that perfect finish that will leave you craving a second piece.

Chocolate Frosting Recipe

Gluten-Free, Dairy-Free, Nut-Free, Soy-Free, Corn-Free

Prep Time: 8 min

Makes: 394 g, Enough for one 8" Cake or 12 Cupcakes

Note: This recipe is Corn-Free as long as you use Corn-Free Powdered Sugar.

Tools

- ✓ Mixer or Beaters
- ✓ Paddle Attachment
- ✓ Whisk or Fine Mesh Metal Strainer
- ✓ Two Bowls
- ✓ Dry Measuring Cups
- ✓ Measuring Spoons
- ✓ Rubber Spatula
- ✓ Metal Spatula or Pastry Bag and Tip to decorate Cupcakes
- ✓ Scale if you have one (for measuring by weight)

Ingredients

- ✓ 2 Tbsp. Rice Milk (31 g) [We recommend Original flavor. Vanilla changes the taste of the frosting.]
- ✓ 1 Tbsp. Water (17 g)
- ✓ 1/4 tsp. Sea Salt (1.3 g)
- ✓ 1/2 cup Palm Shortening (113 g)
- ✓ 1 3/8 cups Powdered Sugar (181 g)
- ✓ 5/8 cup Cocoa (51 g)

Let's Get Mixing

1 Add Sea Salt to Rice Milk and Water. Stir until salt is dissolved and set aside.

2 Sift Powdered Sugar and Cocoa together through metal strainer or use whisk to break up lumps.

3 Cream Palm Oil in mixer with paddle for about a minute on high.

4 Then add half the rice milk/water/salt combo to mixer for about a minute. Start on low so it doesn't splash out. Scrape the bowl with rubber spatula.

5 Add Powdered Sugar/Cocoa half at a time until combined. Mix on low so it doesn't puff out. Add remaining half of rice milk/water/salt. Mix on low and then increase

to high for the last 20 – 30 seconds so it's completely mixed. DON'T OVERMIX AS COLOR WILL CONTINUE TO LIGHTEN.

Tip: If you want the frosting to be softer, you can add a little hot water at the end. Be conservative and just add a teaspoon at a time until you get the consistency you want.

Tip: Keep the frosting at room temperature if you will use it the same day. Or if you want to keep it for future use, you can refrigerate and then bring to room temperature again once you want to frost your chosen dessert.

Chocolate Glaze Recipe

Gluten-Free, Dairy-Free, Nut-Free, Corn-Free

Prep Time: 12 min

Makes: 453 g, Enough for one 8" Cake or 18 Cupcakes

Note: This recipe is Corn-Free as long as you use Corn-Free Powdered Sugar.

Tools

- ✓ Medium Pot
- ✓ Three Bowls
- ✓ Whisk or Fine Mesh Metal Strainer
- ✓ Mixer or Beaters
- ✓ Whip Attachment
- ✓ Dry Measuring Cups
- ✓ Measuring Spoons
- ✓ Liquid Measuring Cup
- ✓ Rubber Spatula
- ✓ Metal Spatula to frost cake or cupcakes
- ✓ Scale if you have one (for measuring by weight)

Ingredients

- ✓ 3 Tbsp. Palm Shortening (34 g)
- ✓ Bittersweet Chocolate (179 g) – about 1 ½ Dark Chocolate bars
- ✓ 3/4 cup Powdered Sugar (111 g)
- ✓ 5/8 cup Original Soy Milk - room temperature (128 g) [Soy Milk works best in this recipe. We recommend Original flavor. Vanilla changes the taste of the glaze.]
- ✓ 1/4 tsp. Salt (1.3 g)

Let's Get Mixing

1 Put 3 cups of water in the pot and bring to a simmer to create a double boiler. Put Shortening and Bittersweet Chips in a mixing bowl and place over the double boiler to melt. Stirring periodically while melting.

2 Measure out Soy Milk and Salt in a separate bowl. Stir until Salt is dissolved and set aside.

3 Sift Powdered Sugar through metal strainer into another bowl or use whisk to remove lumps.

4 Once Chocolate and Shortening are completely melted (but not runny), pour into mixer, use whip attachment. Beat in Soy Milk and Salt until blended on medium speed. Slowly add in the sifted Powdered Sugar 1/3 at a time on low.

5 Beat on high until creamy. Let sit until completely cooled. Once at room temperature, you can smear it on your cakes or cupcakes.

Tip: A metal spatula works best to get a smooth finish on your cake.

Vanilla Frosting Recipe

Gluten-Free, Dairy-Free, Soy-Free, Nut-Free, Corn-Free

Prep Time: 8 min

Makes: 434 g, Enough to frost one 8" Cake or 12 Cupcakes

Note: This recipe is Corn-Free as long as you use Corn-Free Powdered Sugar.

Tools

- ✓ Mixer or Beaters
- ✓ Paddle Attachment
- ✓ Whisk or Fine Mesh Metal Strainer
- ✓ Three Bowls
- ✓ Dry Measuring Cups
- ✓ Liquid Measuring Cup
- ✓ Measuring Spoons
- ✓ Rubber Spatula
- ✓ Metal Spatula to frost cake or Pastry Bag and Tip to decorate cupcakes
- ✓ Scale if you have one (for measuring by weight)

Ingredients

- ✓ 1/3 cup Palm Shortening (81 g)
- ✓ 3/8 tsp. Salt (1.9 g)
- ✓ 2 1/8 cups Powdered Sugar (294 g)
- ✓ 1/4 cup Rice Milk (55 g) [We recommend Original flavor. Vanilla changes the taste of the frosting.]
- ✓ 1 tsp. Vanilla (4 g)

Let's Get Mixing

1 Add Salt to the Rice Milk and stir to dissolve. Set aside.

2 Cream Palm Shortening in the mixer with paddle attachment for about a minute on high.

3 In another bowl, sift Powdered Sugar through a metal strainer if you have one. If not, use a whisk to break up clumps in the Powdered Sugar.

4 Slowly add sifted Powdered Sugar to the Shortening. Alternate with Rice Milk/Salt mixture. Scrape the bowl.

5 Finish by adding Vanilla and beat until creamy and light.
Tip: If you want the frosting to be softer, you can add a little hot water at the end. Be conservative and just add a teaspoon at a time until you get the consistency you want.

6 This frosting can be spread on cake or cupcakes with a metal spatula. Or pipe it on your cupcakes with a pastry bag and tip. Keep it at room temperature if you will use it the same day. Or if you want to keep it for future use, you can refrigerate and then bring to room temperature again once you want to frost your chosen dessert.

Swiss Meringue Buttercream Recipe

Gluten-Free, Dairy-Free, Soy-Free, Nut-Free, Corn-Free

Prep Time: 20 min

Makes: 630 g, More than enough for 8" Cake or 24 Cupcakes

Note: This recipe has uncooked eggs. Pasteurized eggs or a candy thermometer are recommended.

Tools

- ✓ Medium Metal Bowl
- ✓ Medium Pot
- ✓ Whisk
- ✓ Mixer or Beaters
- ✓ Whip Attachment
- ✓ Dry Measuring Cups
- ✓ Liquid Measuring Cup
- ✓ Measuring Spoons
- ✓ Candy Thermometer if your eggs are unpasteurized
- ✓ Rubber Spatula
- ✓ Metal Spatula or Pastry Bag and Tip to decorate Cupcakes
- ✓ Scale if you have one (for measuring by weight)

Ingredients

- ✓ 1/2 cup Egg Whites (113 g) These can be pasteurized liquid egg whites or you can use a candy thermometer to ensure they get hot enough
- ✓ 1 cup + 2 Tbsp. Sugar (227 g)
- ✓ 1/2 tsp. Salt (2.5 g)
- ✓ 1 1/3 cup Palm Shortening – room temperature (283 g)
- ✓ 1 tsp. Vanilla (4 g)

Let's Get Mixing

1 Add 3 cups of water to the pot and bring to a low simmer.

2 Place Egg Whites, Sugar and Salt in bowl and whisk to combine.

3 Set the bowl with Egg Whites, Sugar and Salt over the pot of barely simmering water and heat, whisking constantly until candy thermometer reads 140 - 150°F. If Eggs are already pasteurized, then the temperature isn't crucial. Whisk about 7-8 minutes.

4 Transfer the mixture to mixer. Using the whip attachment, mix on high speed until the meringue is the desired consistency, about four minutes. The peaks should hold their shape when it's finished. It will look like soft marshmallow.

5 Gradually add the Palm Shortening, 1/3 at a time, to the meringue while whipping on high speed. The buttercream should be light and creamy. Blend in the Vanilla as the last step. It should still look like fluffy marshmallow. Beat a final three minutes on high or longer if necessary.

6 You can use the buttercream immediately- smear it on your cakes or cupcakes with a metal spatula. Or pipe it onto your cupcakes with a pastry bag and tip. Keep it at room temperature if you will use the buttercream the same day.

Tip: If you want to keep it for future use, cover and refrigerate it- don't let the plastic touch the top of the buttercream. Bring it to room temperature again once you want to frost your chosen dessert. Once at room temperature, beat the buttercream on the lowest speed with the paddle attachment for about 5 minutes until it's smooth.

Variations on Swiss Meringue Buttercream

Vanilla Cardamom Buttercream

Gluten-Free, Dairy-Free, Soy-Free, Nut-Free, Corn-Free

Prep Time: 20 min

Additional Ingredients

✓ 2 tsp. Cardamom (5 g)

Let's Get Mixing

1 Follow directions for the Swiss Meringue Buttercream.
   Tip: If you want a more mild flavor, start by adding 1 tsp. of Cardamom at a time. Taste and add more if you prefer.

2 When you are adding the Vanilla, also add Cardamom. Mix one final time to get Cardamom evenly distributed throughout the Buttercream.

Dark Chocolate Buttercream

Gluten-Free, Dairy-Free, Nut-Free, Corn-Free

Prep Time: 20 min

Additional Ingredients

✓ 70 g Bittersweet Chocolate (2.5 oz.)

Let's Get Mixing

1 Melt the Bittersweet Chocolate in the microwave or a double boiler. It shouldn't be so hot that it's runny but it should be very creamy.

2 Follow directions for the Swiss Meringue Buttercream. Instead of adding the Vanilla, add the melted Chocolate. Mix one final time to get Chocolate evenly distributed throughout the Buttercream.

Chocolate Lavender Buttercream

Gluten-Free, Dairy-Free, Nut-Free, Corn-Free

Prep Time: 20 min

Additional Ingredients

✓ 70 g Bittersweet Chocolate (2.5 oz.)
✓ 1/2 tsp. Lavender Extract (1.5 g)

Let's Get Mixing

1 Melt the Bittersweet Chocolate in the microwave or a double boiler. It shouldn't be so hot that it's runny but it should be very creamy.

2 Follow directions for the Swiss Meringue Buttercream. Instead of adding the Vanilla, add the melted Chocolate and Lavender. Mix one final time to get Chocolate and Lavender evenly distributed throughout the Buttercream.

Cinnamon Buttercream

Gluten-Free, Dairy-Free, Soy-Free, Nut-Free, Corn-Free

Prep Time: 20 min

Additional Ingredients

✓ 2 tsp. Cinnamon (5.3 g)

Let's Get Mixing

1 Follow directions for the Swiss Meringue Buttercream.
Tip: If you want a more mild flavor, start by adding 1 tsp. of Cinnamon at a time. Taste and add more if you prefer.

2 When you are adding the Vanilla, also add Cinnamon. Mix one final time to get Cinnamon evenly distributed throughout the Buttercream.

Lemon Buttercream

Gluten-Free, Dairy-Free, Soy-Free, Nut-Free, Corn-Free

Prep Time: 20 min

Additional Ingredients

✓ 2 ½ Tbsp. Fresh Lemon Juice (35 g) [1 - 2 Lemons depending on how juicy they are.]

Let's Get Mixing

1 Squeeze the lemon, careful to remove all seeds.

2 Follow directions for the Swiss Meringue Buttercream. Instead of adding the Vanilla, add Lemon Juice. Mix one final time to get Lemon Juice evenly distributed throughout the Buttercream.

Lavender Buttercream

Gluten-Free, Dairy-Free, Soy-Free, Nut-Free, Corn-Free

Prep Time: 20 min

Additional Ingredients

✓ 1 tsp. Lavender Extract (3 g)

Let's Get Mixing

1 Follow directions for the Swiss Meringue Buttercream.
  Tip: If you want a more mild flavor, start by adding 1/2 tsp. of Lavender at a time. Taste and add more if you prefer.

2 Instead of adding the Vanilla, add Lavender extract. Mix one final time to get Lavender evenly distributed throughout the Buttercream.

Pink Velvet Frosting or Buttercream

Gluten-Free, Dairy-Free, Nut-Free, Soy-Free, Corn-Free

Active Prep Time: 13 min - if you use Vanilla Frostingas your base

Active Prep Time: 25 min - if you use Swiss Meringue Buttercream as your base

Passive Prep Time: 45 min

Tools

✓ Medium Pot
✓ Food Processor or Blender
✓ Fine Mesh Metal Strainer
✓ Medium Bowl

Additional Ingredients

✓ 2 medium to large Beets

Let's Get Mixing

1 First prepare the Vanilla Frosting or Swiss Meringue Buttercream as a base for the Pink Velvet topping.

2 To make homemade pink food coloring from scratch, start by boiling the two beets in the pot with the skin on for about 45 minutes or until tender.

3 Put the cooked beets in a food processor (or blender) with a little water to create a moist paste.

4 Strain the beets over a bowl. You can use a metal strainer and press the beets down gently to drain the liquid from them. It won't yield much but you'll get enough dark red juice to make at least one batch of frosting. Be careful, this stuff stains!

5 Go slow and add 1/2 teaspoon of the beet juice at a time to the Vanilla Frosting or Buttercream you've already prepared, until you get the level of pinkness that you like best.

Tip: If you don't have the time to make the pink coloring from scratch, it's always an option to buy coloring. There are some companies making good, all-natural food colorings. Try Maggie's Naturals.

Fillings

Everyone loves taking a bite of cake and discovering that perfectly paired filling or the surprise of a deliciously filled cupcake. In this section we cover a variety of luscious fillings, both traditional and more adventurous, that are perfect for adding that extra layer of flavor to your cakes and cupcakes.

Chocolate Mousse Recipe

Gluten-Free, Dairy-Free, Soy-Free, Nut-Free, Corn-Free

Prep Time: 15 min

Makes: 650 g, Enough to fill in between four layers of 8″ cake rounds, or fill 24 Cupcakes

Note: This recipe has uncooked eggs. Pasteurized eggs are recommended.

Tools

- ✓ Medium Pot
- ✓ Two Bowls
- ✓ Dry Measuring Cups
- ✓ Measuring Spoons
- ✓ Mixer or Beaters
- ✓ Whip Attachment
- ✓ Rubber Spatula
- ✓ Candy Thermometer and Extra Pot if your Eggs are unpasteurized
- ✓ Metal Spatula for frosting cake or Pastry Bag and Bismarck Tip for filling cupcakes
- ✓ Scale if you have one (for measuring by weight)

Ingredients

- ✓ 114 g Unsweetened Baking Chocolate (4 oz.)
- ✓ 3/4 cup Palm Shortening (141 g)
- ✓ 7/8 cup Sugar (190 g)
- ✓ 1 tsp. Vanilla (8 g)
- ✓ 4 Eggs (198 g) Pasteurized

Let's Get Mixing

1 First pasteurize your eggs if necessary.

2 Put three cups of water in the pot and bring to a simmer to create a double boiler.

3 Put Unsweetened Baking Chocolate in a bowl and melt over the double boiler.

4 Cream the Palm Shortening in the mixer with whip attachment. Add the Sugar and Vanilla until combined. Add the melted Chocolate from the double boiler.

5 Beat with the whip attachment until fluffy. Scrape the bowl with the rubber spatula.

6 Add the eggs and beat for three minutes on high until smooth and thick.

7 Let cool to room temperature and then smooth between cake layers. Or cover and refrigerate for later use.

Tip: Fill DreamCups with Chocolate Mousse using Bismarck metal tip and pastry bag.

Favorite Combinations

▷ Sandwiched between layers of Mama Z's Chocolate Cake and frosted with Swiss Meringue Buttercream

▷ Sandwiched between layers of Spiced Banana Cake and frosted with Dark Chocolate Buttercream

Mocha Mousse Recipe

Gluten-Free, Dairy-Free, Soy-Free, Nut-Free, Corn-Free

Prep Time: 15 min

Tools

✓ Spoon measurer
✓ Coffee Grinder

Additional Ingredients

✓ 1 Tbsp. finely ground Espresso Beans (4 g)

Let's Get Mixing

1 Follow all directions for the Chocolate Mousse recipe.

2 Grind a small amount of espresso beans in your coffee grinder. Make sure your grinder is set to the finest espresso grind. You will need 1 Tbsp. ground espresso total.

3 When you add the melted Unsweetened Baking Chocolate to the mixture, also add the ground Espresso. This will give your mousse a little texture, some additional color and a slight caffeine bite!

Tip: If you want to keep the mousse for future use, cover and refrigerate it- don't let the plastic touch the top of the mousse. If drops of condensation form, be careful they don't drip on the surface. Bring the mousse back to room temperature before working with it again.

Vanilla Pastry Cream Recipe

Gluten-Free, Dairy-Free, Soy-Free, Nut-Free, Corn-Free

Prep Time: 15 min

Makes: 718 g, Enough to fill in between four layers of 8″ cake rounds

Note: This recipe has uncooked eggs. Pasteurized eggs are recommended.

Tools

- ✓ Mixer or Beaters
- ✓ Medium Pot
- ✓ Medium Bowl
- ✓ Whip Attachment
- ✓ Whisk
- ✓ Dry Measuring Cups
- ✓ Heatproof Liquid Measuring Cup
- ✓ Rubber Spatula
- ✓ Measuring Spoons
- ✓ Metal Spatula for frosting cake
- ✓ Scale if you have one (for measuring by weight)

Ingredients

- ✓ 2 cups Rice Milk (453 g) [We recommend Original flavor. Vanilla changes the taste of the pastry cream.]
- ✓ 1/4 cup Sugar (51 g)
- ✓ 1/4 tsp. Salt (1.3 g)
- ✓ 5 Egg Yolks (85 g) Pasteurized
- ✓ 1/4 cup Tapioca Flour (28 g)
- ✓ Additional 1/3 cup Sugar (68 g)
- ✓ 2 Tbsp. Palm Shortening - room temperature (28 g)
- ✓ 1 tsp. Vanilla (4 g)

Let's Get Mixing

1 First pasteurize your eggs if necessary.

2 In the medium pot, stir together the Rice Milk, 1/4 cup Sugar and Salt. Bring to a boil over medium heat.

3 In a separate bowl, whisk together the Eggs Yolks.

4 Add the Tapioca and additional 1/3 cup Sugar to the Eggs Yolks. Whisk together until smooth, then add to mixer.

5 When the Rice Milk comes to a boil, drizzle it slowly in the Egg/Sugar/Tapioca mixture in a thin stream while mixing with the whip attachment so that you don't cook the Eggs.
Tip: It's easiest if you put the hot Rice Milk into a heatproof liquid measuring cup with a spout for pouring.

6 Return the entire mixture to the saucepan and slowly bring back to a boil, stirring constantly so the Eggs don't curdle or scorch on the bottom.

7 When the mixture thickens A LOT, in about 3 – 4 minutes, it will look like pudding. Remove from the heat. Add to mixer once again. Use whip attachment on the mixer to add in the Shortening and Vanilla, mixing completely until fully blended.

8 Pour into a heatproof container and place a piece of plastic wrap directly on the surface of the pastry cream to prevent a skin from forming.

9 Refrigerate until completely chilled before using.

Favorite Combinations

▷ Piped into Vanilla Cupcakes to create Cherub DreamCups
▷ Sandwiched between layers of Vanilla Cake and frosted with Dark Chocolate Buttercream
▷ Sandwiched between layers of Spiced Banana Cake and frosted with Chocolate Frosting

Variations on Vanilla Pastry Cream

Lemon Cream

Gluten-Free, Dairy-Free, Soy-Free, Nut-Free, Corn-Free

Prep Time: 16 min

Note: We use Lemon Extract instead of lemon juice because juice makes the pastry cream too runny.

Additional Ingredients

✓ 1 ½ tsp. Lemon Extract (5.3 g)
✓ Zest from One Lemon

Let's Get Mixing

1 Zest the Lemon.

2 Follow all instructions for the Vanilla Pastry Cream. Instead of adding the Vanilla, you will add the Lemon Extract and Lemon Zest.

3 Combine until completely mixed. Pour into a heat-proof container and place a piece of plastic wrap directly on the surface of the cream to prevent a skin from forming.

4 Refrigerate until completely chilled before using.

Raspberry Swirl Cream

Gluten-Free, Dairy-Free, Soy-Free, Nut-Free, Corn-Free

Prep Time: 15 min

Note: This recipe is Corn-Free as long as your Preserves don't have high fructose corn syrup.

Additional Ingredients

✓ 1/3 cup Raspberry Preserves (101 g)

Let's Get Mixing

1 Follow all instructions for the Vanilla Pastry Cream. Instead of adding the Vanilla, you will add the Raspberry Preserves.

2 Combine until completely mixed. Pour into a heat-proof container and place a piece of plastic wrap directly on the surface of the cream to prevent a skin from forming.

3 Refrigerate until completely chilled before using.

Orange Cream

Gluten-Free, Dairy-Free, Soy-Free, Nut-Free, Corn-Free

Prep Time: 17 min

Note: We use Orange Extract instead of orange juice to avoid runniness.

Additional Ingredients

- ✓ 1 ½ tsp. Orange Extract (5.3 g)
- ✓ Zest from Two Medium Oranges

Let's Get Mixing

1 Zest the Oranges.

2 Follow all instructions for the Vanilla Pastry Cream. Instead of adding the Vanilla, you will add the Orange Extract and Orange Zest.

3 Combine until completely mixed. Pour into a heat-proof container and place a piece of plastic wrap directly on the surface of the cream to prevent a skin from forming.

4 Refrigerate until completely chilled before using.

Cardamom Cream

Gluten-Free, Dairy-Free, Soy-Free, Nut-Free, Corn-Free

Prep Time: 15 min

Additional Ingredients

- ✓ 1 ¼ tsp. Cardamom (3.1 g)

Let's Get Mixing

1 Follow all instructions for the Vanilla Pastry Cream. When adding the Vanilla you will also add the Cardamom.

2 Combine until completely mixed. Pour into a heat-proof container and place a piece of plastic wrap directly on the surface of the cream to prevent a skin from forming.

3 Refrigerate until completely chilled before using.

Cinnamon Cream

Gluten-Free, Dairy-Free, Soy-Free, Nut-Free, Corn-Free

Prep Time: 15 min

Additional Ingredients

- ✓ 1 ¾ tsp. Cinnamon (4.7 g)

Let's Get Mixing

1 Follow all instructions for the Vanilla Pastry Cream. When adding the Vanilla you will also add the Cinnamon.

2 Pour into a heat-proof container and place a piece of plastic wrap directly on the surface of the cream to prevent a skin from forming.

3 Refrigerate until completely chilled before using.

Almond Cream

Gluten-Free, Dairy-Free, Soy-Free, Corn-Free

Prep Time: 15 min

Additional Ingredients

- ✓ 2 tsp. Almond Extract (7 g)

Let's Get Mixing

1 Follow all instructions for the Vanilla Pastry Cream. Instead of adding the Vanilla, you will add the Almond Extract.

2 Pour into a heat-proof container and place a piece of plastic wrap directly on the surface of the cream to prevent a skin from forming.

3 Refrigerate until completely chilled before using.

Decorating Tips

In this section, we discuss preparation tips, some tool recommendations and tips for decorating. Learn how to pasteurize your own eggs, frost a pretty cake, fill Dream-Cups (pictured here), keep your cakes moist, speed up your process, use simple but impressive enhancements and add some flare to your decorating.

Pasteurizing Eggs

Uncooked eggs are used in a few of our frostings and fillings. You can easily find either pasteurized liquid or whole eggs in your grocery store. If you prefer to make your own pasteurized eggs instead of buying them, follow these instructions below.

Tools

✓ Candy Thermometer
✓ Small Pot

Let's Get Cooking

1. Using room temperature eggs, fill a small saucepan with water and lower the eggs into the water.
2. Place the saucepan on the stove over medium heat and bring water to 140° to 150° F. It is best to use a thermometer but if you don't have a thermometer, 150° F is when bubbles begin forming on the bottom of the pan.
3. Once the water reaches 140° to 150° F, remove from heat and allow the eggs to rest in the water for three minutes. Your eggs should then be pasteurized.
4. Remove from water and let the eggs cool before using them.

Tips for Decorating

▷ Wrap and refrigerate your cake rounds. Once they are cool, you can slice them lengthwise with a bread knife into thinner rounds for layer cakes.
▷ Use four layers of cake rounds with filling in between each layer for your most decadent cake. This number of layers is still stable but gives a substantial 4″ height.
▷ Wait for your cupcakes or cakes to cool completely before you frost otherwise, the result will be a melted, runny mess.
▷ For added moisture in a layer cake, use simple syrup brushed on your cake layers before you add your filling. This is especially helpful if you've kept your cake rounds refrigerated for a couple of days and they're slightly dry. You can use a brush or spray bottle to apply the simple syrup. Simple syrup recipe:
   – Combine 1 cup of sugar and 2 cups of water. Bring to a boil for approximately 3 minutes. Let cool before using.

▷ If you want to cut down on the amount of work but still want a layer cake, use one of our Swiss Meringue Buttercream Recipes as both the filling AND the frosting.

▷ Pipe any filling or frosting down into a cupcake to create the DreamCups look. Use a long metal tip like the ones for filling Eclairs, these are also called Bismarck metal tips. Poke it in the center of the cupcake. Fill very slowly just until the filling peeks out of the top. You can use Vanilla Pastry Cream (or any variation), Chocolate Mousse, Swiss Meringue Buttercream (or any variation), Vanilla Frosting or Chocolate Frosting.

▷ When frosting a cake, spread a crumb layer first. This is your ugly layer of frosting that no one will see. Then do a final, smooth layer on top of that one to give it a pretty finish.

▷ Metal spatulas work great for getting a nice, smooth frosted finish.

▷ Pastry bags and decorating tips make cupcake decorating go much faster.

▷ Some simple additions to the sides of your cake will make it look upscale. This decorating technique can also conceal some imperfections in your frosting job. Try one of the following add-ons and press them lightly into the sides of your cake:
- Coconut Shavings
- Dark Chocolate Shavings
- Almond Slices
- 1/4″ Chopped Walnuts or Pecans

▷ Try dusting (with a sifter or fine mesh metal strainer) the top of your chocolate cake with powdered sugar or cocoa.

▷ Add some natural coloring to the Swiss Meringue Buttercream or Vanilla Frosting recipes to give your cupcakes some color.

▷ Add a flower to the top of each cupcake. Orchids are always beautiful.

Brownies and Cookies

Who doesn't love a gooey, chocolatey brownie, or a warm cookie just out of the oven? Wasn't that the best feeling as a kid? A warm chocolate chip cookie and glass of cold milk was all it took to make everything right with the world - life was so simple!

Well, it might be a gluten-free cookie and a glass of rice milk these days, but these recipes will give you that same smile and satisfaction.

Dark Chocolate Brownies

The Crave Dark Chocolate Brownie was the very first product I created. In fact, if you read the 'History of Crave' at the beginning of the book, you'll know that this recipe was the one on which Crave was founded. I had been craving brownies since going gluten-free... the delicious, chocolatey, moist brownies that I had eaten my whole life. In 2002, stores simply didn't have good gluten-free desserts, so after much trial and error I finally came up with a recipe that perfectly satisfied my craving. I started serving them to friends who loved them and were shocked to find out these brownies didn't have any wheat or dairy!

Dark Chocolate Brownie Recipe

Gluten-Free, Dairy-Free, Nut-Free, Corn-Free

Prep Time: 18 min, Bake Time: 25 min

Makes: 600 g, Enough for Nine Brownies

Tools

- ✓ Mixer or Beaters
- ✓ Paddle Attachment
- ✓ Medium Pot
- ✓ Three Bowls
- ✓ Dry Measuring Cups
- ✓ Measuring Spoons
- ✓ Rubber Spatula
- ✓ Whisk
- ✓ 8 x 8 Glass Dish or Baking Pan
- ✓ Coffee Grinder if you need to grind Flax Seeds
- ✓ Scale if you have one (for measuring by weight)

Ingredients

- ✓ 1 1/3 cups Bittersweet Chocolate Chips (213 g Bittersweet/Dark Chocolate Bar or 7.5 oz.)
- ✓ 1/3 cup Palm Shortening (63 g)
- ✓ 3/4 cup Sugar (147

bur (60 g)

. ω 350 degrees.

2 Put Chocolate and Shortening over a double boiler. Let sit until completely melted, stirring periodically.

3 Grind Flax Seeds if necessary to make the flax meal.

4 Combine Brown Rice Flour, Flax Meal, Baking Powder and Salt in a large bowl. Whisk out lumps.

5 Once Chocolate is melted, pour into mixer. Turn mixer on low using paddle attachment. Slowly add Sugar until combined. Add Eggs, mix until combined. Add dry ingredients 1/3 at a time, mixing on medium in between. Give bowl a final scrape and mix on medium speed for about 45 seconds, until thoroughly combined.

6 Spray your baking dish or pan evenly. Pour into pan. Smooth top of batter with your rubber spatula until even.
   Tip: The quicker you smooth the brownie batter while it's warm, the easier it will be to spread.

7 Bake for 12 minutes and rotate. Bake for another 13 minutes or until tester comes out clean. Remove from oven and let cool completely before cutting into nine squares.

Variations on Brownies

Toasted Pecan Brownies

Gluten-Free, Dairy-Free, Corn-Free

Prep Time: 19 min, Bake Time: 25 min

A nutty twist on the Dark Chocolate Brownie.

Additional Ingredients

✓ 1/2 cup Pecans (57 g)

Let's Get Baking

1 Chop the Pecans into 1/4″ pieces.

2 Follow all directions for Dark Chocolate Brownie.

3 After all ingredients have been combined, then add most of the Toasted Pecan pieces to brownie batter. Leave a small amount to be sprinkled on the top of the batter. Pat these down gently to make sure the Pecans stick to the top.

4 Follow all baking instructions for the Dark Chocolate Brownie.

Mint Chocolate Chip Brownies

Gluten-Free, Dairy-Free, Nut-Free, Corn-Free

Prep Time: 19 min, Bake Time: 25 min

A little refreshing and rich at the same time. Enough mint to know it's there.

Additional Ingredients

- ✓ 1 ½ teaspoons Peppermint Extract (6 g)
- ✓ 1/2 cup Dairy-Free Dark Chocolate or Semi-Sweet Chips (75 g)

Let's Get Baking

1 Follow all directions for Dark Chocolate Brownie.

2 After all ingredients have been combined, add the Peppermint Extract and Chocolate Chips to brownie batter.

3 Follow all baking instructions for the Dark Chocolate Brownie.

Double Chocolate Brownies

Gluten-Free, Dairy-Free, Nut-Free, Corn-Free

Prep Time: 19 min, Bake Time: 25 min

For those serious chocoholics, for whom the dark chocolate brownie still needs more! Add semi-sweet or dark chocolate chips. Your choice. Make sure your chips are Gluten-Free.

Additional Ingredients

- ✓ 1/2 cup Chocolate Chips (75 g)

Let's Get Baking

1 Follow all directions for Dark Chocolate Brownie.

2 After all ingredients have been combined, then add the Chocolate Chips to brownie batter.

3 Follow all baking instructions for the Dark Chocolate Brownie.

Toasted Coconut Brownies

Gluten-Free, Dairy-Free, Nut-Free, Corn-Free

Prep Time: 21 min, Bake Time: 25 min

A tropical twist on our Dark Chocolate Brownie.

Additional Ingredients

- ✓ 1/2 cup Shredded Coconut (40 g)

Let's Get Baking

1 Toast coconut in the toaster or oven for 2-3 minutes. You should just start to smell the coconut. Pay close attention because they burn fast.

2 Follow all directions for Dark Chocolate Brownie.

3 After all ingredients have been combined, then add the Toasted Coconut to the brownie batter.

4 Follow all baking instructions for the Dark Chocolate Brownie.

❋ ❋ ❋

utter Brownies

-Free

min, Bake Time: 25 min

recipes in our book that has dairy only because, at
lishing, you can't find all-natural, gluten-free and
t butter chips. So, if you can tolerate peanuts and
dairy, this is a sinful combination of peanut butter

Additional Ingredients

✓ 1/2 cup of Peanut Butter Chips (75 g)

Let's Get Baking

1 Follow all directions for Dark Chocolate Brownie.

2 After all ingredients have been combined, add the Peanut Butter Chips to the brownie batter.

3 Follow all baking instructions for the Dark Chocolate Brownie.

Monster Cookies

Gluten-Free, Dairy-Free, Corn-Free

This cookie is like a Blondie with Chocolate Chunks. It has a soft, buttery taste despite having no dairy. We've been told it tastes like a baked version of cookie dough (if that makes any sense!). For several years we had a very sweet man order 50 of these at a time for his twin sons with numerous food allergies. We would hear from him every couple of months: this was the boys' primary dessert and they loved it, even demanded it he told us. Hey Karl, you can make these at home now!!

Monster Cookie Recipe

Gluten-Free, Dairy-Free, Corn-Free

Prep Time: 15 min, Bake Time: 30 min

Makes: 533 g, Enough for Nine Bar Cookies

Tools

- ✓ Mixer or Beaters
- ✓ Paddle Attachment
- ✓ Two Bowls
- ✓ Dry Measuring Cups
- ✓ Measuring Spoons
- ✓ Whisk
- ✓ Rubber Spatula
- ✓ 8 x 8 Glass Dish or Baking Pan
- ✓ Scale if you have one (for measuring by weight)

Ingredients

- ✓ 3/4 cup Brown Rice Flour (113 g)
- ✓ 1/4 cup Almond Meal (23 g)
- ✓ 3/4 tsp. Baking Powder (2 g)
- ✓ 1/2 tsp. Salt (2.5 g)
- ✓ 1/8 tsp. Xanthan Gum (.3 g)
- ✓ Pinch of Cinnamon
- ✓ 1/4 cup Brown Sugar (43 g)
- ✓ 1/2 cup Sugar (102 g)
- ✓ 1/2 cup Palm Shortening (94 g)
- ✓ 1 Tbsp. Applesauce (17 g)
- ✓ 1 Egg (50 g)
- ✓ 1/3 cup Semi-Sweet or Dark Chocolate Chips (62 g) + 2 Tbsp. to sprinkle on top (23 g)
- ✓ Gluten Free Baking Spray

Let's Get Baking

1 Preheat oven to 350 degrees.

2 Combine all dry ingredients in a medium bowl. Brown Rice Flour, Almond Meal, Baking Powder, Salt, Xanthan Gum and Cinnamon. Whisk out lumps.

65

3 Combine the two Sugars, Shortening and Applesauce in mixer. Beat until creamy on medium speed. Beat in Egg on high until fluffy.

4 Slowly add the whisked dry ingredients to the wet ingredients, half at a time. Beat until combined on medium. Scrape bowl and mix on high for a final 30 seconds. Mix in 1/3 cup Chocolate Chips and get them evenly distributed throughout the dough.

5 Spray dish with an even mist. Use the rubber spatula to spread the cookie dough evenly.

   Tip: Lots of variables can change your bake time. The best way to determine the bake time in your environment is to be conservative.

6 Bake for 12 minutes, rotate and bake for another 13 minutes. Take out and sprinkle remaining chocolate chips on top. Place back in oven and bake for another 5 minutes.

7 Cookies are fully baked with the top is golden brown. Remove from oven and let cool completely before cutting into nine squares.

Variations on Monster Cookies

Nutty Monster Cookies

Gluten-Free, Dairy-Free, Corn-Free

Prep Time: 16 min, Bake Time: 30 min

While there is already some almond meal in this cookie bar, there are no chunky nuts. Walnuts in this cookie are a great combination with the chocolate chips.

Additional Ingredients

   ✓ 1/4 cup Walnut pieces, chopped into ¼" pieces (30 g)

Let's Get Baking

1 Follow all directions in the Monster Cookie recipe.

2 When adding Chocolate Chips, add Walnut pieces too.

3 Follow all baking instructions for the Monster Cookie.

Peanut Butter Chocolate Monster Cookies

Gluten-Free, Corn-Free

Prep Time: 16 min, Bake Time: 30 min

One of the few recipes in our book that has dairy only because, at the time of publishing, you can't find all-natural, gluten-free and dairy-free peanut butter chips. So, if you can tolerate peanuts and you can tolerate dairy, this is a sinful combination of peanut butter and chocolate!

Additional Ingredients

✓ 1/4 cup Peanut Butter Chips (38 g)

Let's Get Baking

1 Follow all directions in the Monster Cookie recipe.

2 When adding the Chocolate Chips, add Peanut Butter Chips too.

3 Follow all baking instructions for the Monster Cookie.

Peanut Butter Monster Cookies

Gluten-Free, Corn-Free

Prep Time: 16 min, Bake Time: 30 min

The full-on peanut butter version, no chocolate.

Additional Ingredients

✓ 1/3 cup Peanut Butter Chips (50 g)

Let's Get Baking

1 Follow all directions in the Monster Cookie recipe.

2 Leave out the Chocolate Chips and add Peanut Butter Chips instead.

3 Follow all baking instructions for the Monster Cookie.

"Oatmeal" Raisin Cookies

Gluten-Free, Dairy-Free, Soy-Free, Corn-Free

When Crave opened, it was still generally accepted in the GF community that all oats were gluten contaminated. Our solution to this problem- we developed a recipe with a workaround that created an oatmeal texture using almond meal and shredded coconut instead of oats. These days you can find oats that are safe but we still like the chewy, flavorful result of our non-oat version.

"Oatmeal" Raisin Cookie Recipe

Gluten-Free, Dairy-Free, Soy-Free, Corn-Free

Prep Time: 15 min, Bake Time: 10 min

Makes: 608 g, Enough for 24 Cookies

Note: This recipe is Corn-Free as long as your Applesauce has no high fructose corn syrup.

Tools

- ✓ Mixer or Beaters
- ✓ Paddle Attachment
- ✓ Two Bowls
- ✓ Rubber Spatula
- ✓ Dry Measuring Cups
- ✓ Measuring Spoons
- ✓ Whisk
- ✓ Baking Sheet
- ✓ Coffee Grinder if you need to grind Flax Seeds
- ✓ Scale if you have one (for measuring by weight)

Ingredients

- ✓ 1/2 cup +3 Tbsp. Brown Rice Flour (103 g)
- ✓ 1/2 tsp. Baking Powder (1.3 g)
- ✓ 3/8 tsp. Salt (1.9 g)
- ✓ 3/4 tsp. Cinnamon (1.8 g)
- ✓ 1/4 tsp. Nutmeg (1 g)
- ✓ 1/8 tsp. Allspice (.3 g)
- ✓ 2 ½ Tbsp. Flax Meal (24 g)
- ✓ 1 Egg (50 g)
- ✓ 2 Tbsp. Applesauce (33 g)
- ✓ 3 Tbsp. Almond Meal (17 g)
- ✓ 1/4 tsp. Baking Soda (1.3 g)
- ✓ 5/8 cup Palm Shortening (141 g)
- ✓ 5/8 cup Sugar (125 g) [you can also use Sucanat or unrefined sugar if you prefer]
- ✓ 3/8 cup Shredded Coconut (33 g)
- ✓ 1/2 cup Raisins (75 g)
- ✓ Gluten Free Baking Spray or Parchment Paper

Let's Get Baking

1 Preheat oven to 350 degrees.

2 Measure out all dry ingredients- Brown Rice Flour, Baking Powder, Salt, Cinnamon, Nutmeg and Allspice. Whisk together to break up any clumps and set aside.

3 Grind Flax Seeds if necessary to make the Flax Meal.

4 In mixer, beat Flax Meal, Egg, Applesauce, Almond Meal and Baking Soda with paddle attachment on low.

5 Add Shortening and Sugar into mixer until well combined. Beat on low.

6 Slowly add whisked dry ingredients, half at a time. Mix on low and then medium until fully combined.
Tip: Break up the Raisins that are stuck together before adding to the dough.

7 Fold in Coconut, then Raisins. Beat on low. Scrape bowl with rubber spatula and mix one last time until Coconuts and Raisins are evenly distributed.

8 Line baking sheets with parchment paper or spray lightly with oil.

9 Scoop rounded Tablespoon (25 g) balls of the cookie dough onto the baking sheet. Feel free to drop larger scoops for bigger cookies.

10 Bake for 8 – 10 minutes until edges are golden and cookies are set. Remove and cool to room temperature before wrapping and storing.

Variations on "Oatmeal" Raisin Cookies

"Oatmeal" Chocolate Chip Cookies

Gluten-Free, Dairy-Free, Corn-Free

Prep Time: 15 min, Bake Time: 10 min

Good old Oatmeal Chocolate Chip. We love the combination of the spices and chocolate chips in this recipe. Slightly more decadent than the "Oatmeal" Raisin.

Additional Ingredients

 ✓ 1/2 cup Dairy-Free Dark Chocolate or Semi-Sweet Chips (75 g)

Let's Get Baking

1 Follow all directions for "Oatmeal" Raisin Cookies, but instead of adding 1/2 cup of Raisins, add 1/2 cup of Chocolate Chips.

2 Follow all baking instructions for the "Oatmeal" Raisin Cookie.

Trail Mix Cookies

Gluten-Free, Dairy-Free, Soy-Free, Corn-Free

Prep Time: 15 min, Bake Time: 10 min

These are a protein filled, healthy snack on the trail or off!

Additional Ingredients

- ✓ 1/4 cup Chopped Apricots, 1/4" pieces (50 g)
- ✓ 1/4 cup Chopped Walnuts, 1/4" pieces (30 g)

Let's Get Baking

1 Follow all directions for "Oatmeal" Raisin Cookies, but instead of adding the full 1/2 cup of Raisins, only add the 1/4 cup Raisins. Also add the Apricots and the Walnuts.

2 Follow all baking instructions for the "Oatmeal" Raisin Cookie.

Tarts

Tarts! Such a beautiful, delicate, extravagant dessert; this is the dessert you serve at a dinner party when you feel like impressing! Getting the gluten-free pastry recipe just right was one of my greater challenges.

But now that you have our recipe, you can fill it with one of the many flavors and fruit fillings in this chapter or create your own for that perfectly impressive dessert.

Pastry

Gluten-Free, Dairy-Free, Nut-Free, Soy-Free, Corn-Free

I missed pastry so much when I went gluten-free! I went through many different versions to get it just right. The goal was a buttery, flaky, light pastry that tasted like nothing was missing. Despite being dairy-free, as Kelly Courson of Celiac Chicks says, 'It tastes like it's full of butter!". This recipe works really well for tarts, pies, even quiche.

Pastry Recipe

Gluten-Free, Dairy-Free, Nut-Free, Soy-Free, Corn-Free

Prep Time: 15 min, Bake Time: 25 min

Makes: 722 g, Enough for Eight 4" Tart Crusts or Three 8" - 9" Tart Crusts

Tools

- ✓ Mixer or Beaters
- ✓ Paddle Attachment
- ✓ Dry Measuring Cups
- ✓ Measuring Spoons
- ✓ Whisk
- ✓ Rubber Spatula
- ✓ Two Bowls
- ✓ Paring knife
- ✓ Cutting Board
- ✓ Tart Pans
- ✓ Scale if you have one (for measuring by weight)

Ingredients

- ✓ 1 cup Palm Shortening (shortening should be cold) 227 g
- ✓ 1 1/3 cup Sweet Rice Flour (221 g)
- ✓ 1/3 cup + 2 Tbsp. Potato Starch (79 g)
- ✓ 1/4 cup Tapioca Flour (28 g)
- ✓ 1 Tbsp. + 1 tsp. Xanthan Gum (8 g)
- ✓ 1/2 tsp. Salt (2.5 g)
- ✓ 1/4 cup Sugar (57 g)
- ✓ 2 Eggs (99 g)
- ✓ Gluten Free Baking Spray

Let's Get Baking

1 Cut the cold shortening into small pieces. Add to the mixer.

2 In a separate bowl, combine all dry ingredients- Sweet Rice Flour, Potato Starch, Tapioca Flour, Xanthan Gum, Salt and Sugar. Whisk to break up any clumps. Slowly add the dry ingredients into the mixer half at a time so they don't puff out. Mix briefly until combined. Scrape the bowl with the rubber spatula.

3 Add the Eggs. Mix only until combined. Don't overmix or you will smooth out all the Shortening chunks. Scrape the bowl and mix a final 30 seconds on medium.

4 If pastry is too soft to work with, refrigerate before using.

5 Spray your pans lightly.

6 Once pastry is firm enough, cut off enough for the size of your chosen tart pan.
   ▷ Approximately 240 g for 8 – 9″ pans.
   ▷ Approximately 90 g for 4″ pans.
   Tip: Flour your hands (or wet them with a little water) so the pastry doesn't stick to you.

7 Using your fingers, press the dough down into the pan, starting at the center and working your way out to the edges. The dough should be no more than 1/4″ thick. Now your pastry is ready for the Lemon, Pumpkin or the Frangipane Tarts.

8 If you are blind baking the pastry to prepare if for the Fresh Fruit Tart, preheat oven to 350 degrees. Line the pastry with pie weights to keep it from puffing up during baking.
   Tip: If you don't have pie weights, you can use dried beans instead. Line pastry with aluminum foil first so the beans don't stick to the pastry.

9 Bake about 12 minutes and rotate. Bake another 13 minutes or until the pastry turns golden brown. Let the pastry cool completely, then refrigerate. Once it's completely refrigerated and cooled, then remove it from the pan by gently flipping it over onto a flat surface. Now it's ready to be filled with pastry cream and fruit.

Pumpkin Tart

Gluten-Free, Dairy-Free, Soy-Free, Nut-Free, Corn-Free

This is such a traditional dessert and a real holiday favorite - a Fall treat that a lot of folks with allergies or Celiac Disease missed terribly! All this tart business started with the Pumpkin Tart in 2006 when one of our customers asked us to create a Gluten-Free, Dairy-Free Pumpkin Tart for Thanksgiving. So, first came the pastry and then the pumpkin filling. I wanted the spice level perfect and the pumpkin texture smooth and creamy. Add a little dairy-free whipped topping to finish it off.

Pumpkin Tart Recipe

Gluten-Free, Dairy-Free, Soy-Free, Nut-Free, Corn-Free

Prep Time: 10 min, Bake Time: 50 min

Makes: 717 g, Enough for One 8″ – 9″ Pumpkin Tart

Tools

- ✓ Mixer or Beaters
- ✓ Whip Attachment
- ✓ Two Bowls
- ✓ Dry Measuring Cups
- ✓ Liquid Measuring Cup
- ✓ Measuring Spoons
- ✓ Rubber Spatula
- ✓ Scale if you have one (for measuring by weight)

Ingredients

- ✓ 3/8 tsp. Salt (1.9 g)
- ✓ 3/4 tsp. Cinnamon (1.8 g)
- ✓ 3/4 tsp. Ginger (1.8 g)
- ✓ 3/8 tsp. Allspice (.9 g)
- ✓ 1/4 tsp. Nutmeg (.4 g)
- ✓ 1 1/3 cup Pumpkin (319 g) – (This is 3/4 can of 15 oz. canned Pumpkin)
- ✓ 3 Eggs (153 g)
- ✓ 3/4 cup Rice Milk (170 g) [We recommend Original flavor. Vanilla changes the taste of the filling.]
- ✓ 1/3 cup Sugar (68 g)

Let's Get Baking

1 Make your Pastry in advance.

2 Preheat oven to 350 degrees.

3 Combine all dry ingredients - Salt, Cinnamon, Ginger, Allspice and Nutmeg. Whisk to remove any clumps.

4 Combine Pumpkin and Eggs in mixer using whip attachment. Once fully combined, add Rice Milk.

5 Add all Sugar and mix on medium. Slowly add dry ingredients, half at a time, until combined. Scrape bowl and mix one final time on high to get it thoroughly mixed-

about 30 seconds.

Tip: At this point, you have the option to brush the raw tart shell with egg white. The egg white acts as glue and ensures that the filling doesn't pull away from the tart crust. This step gives a cleaner finished look.

6 Pour Pumpkin filling into prepared, raw tart shell. This recipe should be enough for at least one large Pumpkin Tart.

7 Bake for 25 minutes, rotate and bake for another 25 minutes. Or until the crust is golden brown and the center of the filling looks set. You can also insert a tester to see if it comes out clean.

8 Let the tart cool completely, then refrigerate. Once the tart is completely refrigerated and cooled, then remove it from the pan.

Tip: To remove the tart from the pan, place a cutting board over the top of the cooled pastry. Hold the tart firm to the cutting board and flip it over. Pull the tart pan off the bottom. Replace the pan with a plate on which you want to serve the tart. Flip it back over and remove the cutting board from the top so that the tart is now right side up on the plate instead of in the pan.

9 Refrigerate the finished tart until 30 minutes before you serve. Let the pastry come to room temperature for best taste and texture.

Lemon Tart

Gluten-Free, Dairy-Free, Soy-Free, Nut-Free, Corn-Free

Our Lemon Tart was one of our most popular products. People loved the light, tangy sweetness of this little tart. They are just so darn cute too! We recommend serving it with a dairy-free whipped cream and/or blueberries... perfect for a summer dessert.

Lemon Tart Recipe

Gluten-Free, Dairy-Free, Soy-Free, Nut-Free, Corn-Free

Prep Time: 10 min

Makes: 695 g, Enough for Nine 4″ Tarts

Tools

- ✓ Mixer or Beaters
- ✓ Whip Attachment
- ✓ Two Bowls
- ✓ Dry Measuring Cups
- ✓ Liquid Measuring Cup
- ✓ Measuring Spoons
- ✓ Whisk
- ✓ Lemon Squeezer
- ✓ Baking Sheets
- ✓ Ladle

Ingredients

- ✓ 2/3 cup Lemon Juice (142 g) [4 - 5 Lemons depending on how juicy they are.]
- ✓ 5 Eggs (255 g)
- ✓ 1/3 cup Rice Milk (85 g) [We recommend Original flavor. Vanilla changes the taste of the filling.]
- ✓ 1 cup Sugar (213 g)

Let's Get Baking

1 Make your Pastry in advance.

2 Preheat oven to 350 degrees.

3 Squeeze the lemons, careful to remove the seeds.

4 Combine Lemon Juice, Eggs and Rice Milk in mixer. Use whip attachment to whip on medium speed until combined.

5 Add Sugar and mix on medium until fully combined.
   Tip: At this point, you have the option to brush the raw tart shells with egg white. The egg white acts as glue and ensures that the filling doesn't pull away from the tart crust. It also keeps the lemon from soaking into the crust as much.

6 Place all 4″ Tart Shells on baking sheets. The filling will be somewhat runny, so it's best to ladle directly into each prepared, raw pastry shell.

7 Fill shells with 77 g of Lemon Filling. You will have enough filling for nine tarts. Leave enough room in each tart shell so the filling doesn't slosh over when you're placing them in the oven.

8 Bake about 15 minutes and rotate. Bake another 20 minutes or until the crust is golden brown and the filling looks set.

9 Let the tart cool completely, then refrigerate. Once the tart is completely refrigerated and cooled, then remove it from the pan.
   Tip: To remove the tart from the pan, place a cutting board over the top of the cooled pastry. Hold the tart firm to the cutting board and flip it over. Pull the tart pan off the bottom. Replace the pan with a plate on which you want to serve the tart. Flip it back over and remove the cutting board from the top so that the tart is now right side up on the plate instead of in the pan.

10 Cover with plastic wrap. Refrigerate until 30 minutes before you serve. Let the pastry come to room temperature for best taste and texture.

Apple and Apricot Frangipane Tarts

Gluten-Free, Dairy-Free, Soy-Free, Corn-Free

The Apple and Apricot Frangipane Tarts were fraternal twins. After Pumpkin and Lemon Tarts, a customer asked us to create Apple too. We wanted to make this tart more upscale so we added our frangipane topping to give it some extra flare. Frangipane is a sweet, delicate European almond filling. Apricot tagged along in the process and they were born at the same time and with equal love.

Frangipane Recipe

Gluten-Free, Dairy-Free, Soy-Free, Corn-Free

Prep Time: 10 min

Makes: 485 g, Enough for Eight 4″ Tarts or One 8 - 9″ Tart

Tools

- ✓ Mixer or Beaters
- ✓ Paddle Attachment
- ✓ Dry Measuring Cups
- ✓ Measuring Spoons
- ✓ Rubber Spatula
- ✓ Scale if you have one (for measuring by weight)

Ingredients

- ✓ 2/3 cup Palm Shortening (125 g)
- ✓ 5/8 cup Sugar (125 g)
- ✓ 2 Eggs (99 g)
- ✓ 3/4 cup Almond Meal (125 g)
- ✓ 2 ½ tsp. Brown Rice Flour (8 g)
- ✓ 3/4 tsp. Almond Extract (3 g)

Let's Get Mixing

1 Cream the Palm Shortening and Sugar together with paddle until light and fluffy on medium speed and then increase to high just until combined.

2 Beat in the Eggs one at a time on medium speed.

3 Scrape the bowl with the rubber spatula. Then fold in the Almond Meal and Brown Rice Flour to form a smooth paste. Mix until just combined.

4 Beat in Almond Extract last.

5 Your frangipane is now ready for your Apple or Apricot Frangipane Tart.

Apricot Frangipane Tart Recipe

Gluten-Free, Dairy-Free, Soy-Free, Corn-Free

Prep Time: 8 min, Bake Time: 35 min

Makes: Enough for Eight 4″ Tarts or One 8 - 9″ Tart

Note: This recipe is Corn-Free as long as you use Apricot Preserves without high fructose corn syrup.

Tools

- ✓ Measuring Spoons
- ✓ Dry Measuring Cups
- ✓ One or Two Baking Sheets
- ✓ Pastry Bag for Piping Frangipane OR Spoon
- ✓ Scale if you have one (for measuring by weight)

Ingredients

- ✓ 7/8 cup Apricot preserves (200 g)

Let's Get Baking

1 Follow directions for the Pastry and Frangipane. Then deposit the Apricot preserves as directed below.

2 Preheat oven to 350 degrees.

3 Once your pastry pans are prepared, fill each 4″ raw pastry shell with 1/4 cup of Frangipane (or pipe 47 g with pastry bag). Then dollop 1 ¾ Tbsp. Apricot Preserves (or pipe 25 g) right on top, in the center of the frangipane.

   ▷ Or just use all of Apricot preserves and Frangipane at once if you are making one large tart. Frangipane goes directly into the raw, pastry shell and then the Apricot Preserves centered, on top.

4 Place all tart pans on baking sheets. Bake for 20 minutes and rotate. Bake for another 15 minutes or until frangipane and pastry are golden brown. You may need to bake slightly longer for an 8 - 9″ Tart.

5 Let the tart cool completely, then refrigerate. Once the tart is completely refrigerated and cooled, then remove it from the pan.
   Tip: To remove the tart from the pan, place a cutting board over the top of the cooled pastry. Hold the tart firm to the cutting board and flip it over. Pull the tart pan off the bottom. Replace the pan with a plate on which you want to serve the tart. Flip it back over and remove the cutting board from the top so that the tart is now right side up on the plate instead of in the pan.

6 Refrigerate the finished tart until 30 minutes before you serve. Let the pastry come to room temperature for best taste and texture.

❊ ❊ ❊

Apple Frangipane Tart Recipe

Gluten-Free, Dairy-Free, Soy-Free, Corn-Free

Prep Time: 10 min, Bake Time: 45 min

Makes: Enough for Eight 4″ Tarts or One 8″ – 9″ Tart

Tools

- ✓ Medium Bowl
- ✓ Large Spoon for Mixing Apples
- ✓ Cutting Board
- ✓ Knife
- ✓ Measuring Spoons
- ✓ Dry Measuring Cups
- ✓ One or Two Baking Sheets
- ✓ Pastry Bag for Piping Frangipane OR Spoon
- ✓ Scale if you have one (for measuring by weight)

Ingredients

- ✓ 2 medium Granny Smith Apples or 316 g chopped apples
- ✓ 1 Tbsp. Sugar (14 g)
- ✓ 1/2 tsp. Cinnamon (1 g)

Let's Get Baking

1 Follow directions for the Pastry and Frangipane.

2 Preheat oven to 350 degrees.

3 Core the apples and chop into 1/2″ pieces. We use Granny Smith's because they're tart and juicy. Mix chopped Apples with Sugar and Cinnamon in a bowl.

4 Once your pastry pans are prepared, fill each 4″ raw pastry shell with 3 Tbsp. (40 g) of Apple mix first. Then use pastry bag to pipe or dollop 1/4 cup of Frangipane (or 47 g) around the Apples.
   ▷ Or just use all of Apple and Frangipane at once if you are making one large tart. Put Apples in pastry shell first and then spread Frangipane on top.

5 Place all tart pans on baking sheets. Bake for 20 minutes and rotate. Bake for another 20 - 25 minutes, until frangipane and pastry are golden brown. You may need to bake slightly longer for an 8″ - 9″ Tart.

6 Let the tart cool completely, then refrigerate. Once the tart is completely refrigerated and cooled, then remove it from the pan.

Tip: To remove the tart from the pan, place a cutting board over the top of the cooled pastry. Hold the tart firm to the cutting board and flip it over. Pull the tart pan off the bottom. Replace the pan with a plate on which you want to serve the tart. Flip it back over and remove the cutting board from the top so that the tart is now right side up on the plate instead of in the pan.

7 Refrigerate the finished tart until 30 minutes before you serve. Let the pastry come to room temperature for best taste and texture.

Fresh Fruit Tarts

Gluten-Free, Dairy-Free, Soy-Free, Nut-Free, Corn-Free

What's the best summer dessert? A light, cool tart with fresh summer fruit! These are so pretty and easy to make ahead of time for a dinner party. Use any summer fruit that's in season and looks the best at the market! We've provided our favorite combinations in this section.

Fresh Blueberry Tart Recipe

Gluten-Free, Dairy-Free, Soy-Free, Nut-Free, Corn-Free

Prep Time: 5 min

Makes: Enough for Eight 4″ Tarts or One 8″ - 9″ Tart

Tools

✓ Pastry Bag for piping Pastry Cream or Spoon

Additional Ingredients

✓ 1 lb of Blueberries

Let's Get Baking

1 Bake Tart Shell and make Pastry Cream ahead of time.

2 With baked and cooled tart shells ready, add the refrigerated pastry cream to the tart shell. Fill each tart shell about 2/3 full of pastry cream (70 g for 4″ Tart Shells).

3 Finish by covering the top of the pastry cream with fresh blueberries, about 55 g.

4 Refrigerate until 30 minutes before serving for softer pastry. Or serve cold, if you prefer colder fruit/cream.

Sweet Strawberry Tart Recipe

Gluten-Free, Dairy-Free, Soy-Free, Nut-Free, Corn-Free

Prep Time: 8 min

Makes: Enough for Eight 4″ Tarts or One 8″ - 9″ Tart

Tools

- ✓ Pastry Bag for piping Pastry Cream or Spoon
- ✓ Paring Knife
- ✓ Cutting Board

Additional Ingredients

- ✓ 16 large, sweet Strawberries

Let's Get Baking

1 Bake Tart Shell and make Pastry Cream ahead of time.

2 With baked and cooled tart shells ready, add the refrigerated pastry cream to the tart shell. Fill each tart shell about 2/3 full of pastry cream (70 g for 4″ Tart Shells).

3 Slice up your sweet strawberries. Fan them out in a pretty arrangement on top of the pastry cream.

4 Refrigerate until 30 minutes before serving for softer pastry. Or serve cold, if you prefer colder fruit/cream.

Summer Peach Tart Recipe

Gluten-Free, Dairy-Free, Soy-Free, Nut-Free, Corn-Free

Prep Time: 8 min

Makes: Enough for Eight 4″ Tarts or One 8″ - 9″ Tart

Tools

- ✓ Pastry Bag for piping Pastry Cream or Spoon
- ✓ Paring Knife
- ✓ Cutting Board

Additional Ingredients

- ✓ 4 medium, ripe Peaches

Let's Get Baking

1 Bake Tart Shell and make Pastry Cream ahead of time.

2 With baked and cooled tart shells ready, add the refrigerated pastry cream to the tart shell. Fill each tart shell about 2/3 full of pastry cream (70 g for 4″ Tart Shells).

3 Slice up the peaches. Fan them out in a pretty arrangement on top of pastry cream. About 1/2 peach per tart.

4 Refrigerate until 30 minutes before serving for softer pastry. Or serve cold, if you prefer colder fruit/cream.

Favorite Combinations

- ▷ Almond Pastry Cream/Fresh Blueberry
- ▷ Cardamom Pastry Cream/Summer Peach
- ▷ Lemon Pastry Cream/Sweet Strawberry

Muffins

Muffin tops (and bottoms for that matter!) in lots of moist, delicious flavors. Muffins can be snacks, dessert or breakfast.

Enjoy this versatile, portable, yummy, hand-sized food any time of the day.

Muffin Base

Gluten-Free, Dairy-Free, Soy-Free, Nut-Free, Corn-Free

This recipe is a great, dependable base for more adventurous muffin variations. We've made some recommendations in this section that you can use as a starting point for your own experimentation. Make them as healthy, or alternatively, as decadent as you want. Moist muffins for breakfast, desserts, snacks... yum!

Muffin Base Recipe

Gluten-Free, Dairy-Free, Soy-Free, Nut-Free, Corn-Free

Prep Time: 15 min, Bake Time: 20 min

Makes: 801 g, Enough for 12 Muffins

Tools

- ✓ Mixer or Beaters
- ✓ Paddle Attachment
- ✓ Two Bowls
- ✓ Rubber Spatula
- ✓ Whisk
- ✓ Dry Measuring Cups
- ✓ Liquid Measuring Cup
- ✓ Measuring Spoons
- ✓ Muffin Pans
- ✓ Muffin Papers or Gluten Free Baking Spray
- ✓ Scale if you have one (for measuring by weight)

Ingredients

- ✓ 1/2 cup Palm Shortening (113 g)
- ✓ 1 cup Sugar (210 g)
- ✓ 2 Eggs (99 g)
- ✓ 2 tsp. Vanilla (8 g)
- ✓ 3 Tbsp. Tapioca Flour (20 g)
- ✓ 3/4 cup Sweet Rice Flour (119 g)
- ✓ 1/2 cup + 1 Tbsp. Potato Starch (102 g)
- ✓ 2 tsp. Baking Powder (5.4 g)
- ✓ 1/2 tsp. Baking Soda (2.7 g)
- ✓ 3/4 tsp. Xanthan Gum (1.5 g)
- ✓ 1/4 tsp. Salt (1.3 g)
- ✓ 1/2 cup Rice Milk (119 g) [We recommend Original flavor. Vanilla changes the taste of the batter.]

Let's Get Baking

1 Preheat oven to 350 degrees.

2 Beat Shortening and Sugar for three minutes on high with paddle attachment until fluffy.

3 Scrape bowl, add Egg and Vanilla, and beat another two minutes on high.

4 Whisk together the dry ingredients- Tapioca Flour, Sweet Rice Flour, Potato Starch, Baking Powder, Baking Soda, Xanthan Gum and Salt. Whisk until lumps disappear.

5 Alternate adding the whisked dry ingredients with Rice Milk into the mixer, half of each at a time.

6 Beat until smooth and fully combined. About 2 minutes.

7 Spray your muffin pans or use muffin papers.

8 Fill each muffin cup or paper nearly full with batter (or 66 g). This makes about 12 muffins.

9 Bake for 10 minutes, rotate and bake for another 10 minutes. Remove from oven when tester comes out clean.

10 Let cool and remove from pan.

Tip: Take notes whenever you discover something that works slightly better. Maybe you want it baked for a longer or shorter time or prefer a stronger flavor. Whatever it is, make a note for next time so you can create a version suited to your specific taste.

Variations on Muffin Base

Cherry Almond Muffins

Gluten-Free, Dairy-Free, Soy-Free, Corn-Free

Prep Time: 17 min, Bake Time: 20 min

The almond and cherries in this recipe are not overly sweet and the almond slices give it a nice, finished look.

Additional Ingredients

- ✓ 1/2 cup Dried Cherries (75 g)
- ✓ 1 tsp. Almond Extract (4 g)
- ✓ 1/4 cup Almond Slices for garnish - optional (22 g)

Let's Get Baking

1 Follow all directions for the Muffin Base recipe.
Tip: Break apart any clumps of Cherries sticking together before you add them to the batter. This will ensure they will be distributed evenly when mixed.

2 Once you have mixed all the dry ingredients and Rice Milk, add the Cherries and Almond Extract into the batter. Mix one last time until everything is fully combined and the Cherries are evenly distributed.

3 Follow all baking instructions for the Muffin Base.

Tip: Bake 10 minutes, remove from oven. Sprinkle the almond slices on top of each muffin for garnish. The batter should still be wet enough for the almonds to stick to the top. Replace and bake for the final 10 minutes.

Cranberry Orange Muffins

Gluten-Free, Dairy-Free, Soy-Free, Nut-Free, Corn-Free

Prep Time: 17 min, Bake Time: 20 min

A fruity, zesty muffin for breakfast.

Additional Ingredients

- ✓ 1/2 cup Dried Cranberries (75 g)
- ✓ 1 tsp. Orange Extract (4 g)
- ✓ Zest from One Medium Orange

Let's Get Baking

1 Follow all directions for the Muffin Base recipe.
Tip: Break apart any clumps of Cranberries sticking together before you add them to the batter. This will ensure they will be distributed evenly when mixed.

2 Once you have mixed all the dry ingredients and Rice Milk, add the Cranberries, Orange Extract and Orange Zest into the batter. Mix one last time until everything is fully combined and the Cranberries are evenly distributed.

3 Follow all baking instructions for the Muffin Base.

Lemon Zest Muffins

Gluten-Free, Dairy-Free, Soy-Free, Nut-Free, Corn-Free

Prep Time: 18 min, Bake Time: 20 min

This light, sweet muffin is so fluffy and slightly tart. Simple and really satisfying.

Additional Ingredients

- ✓ 1/3 cup Fresh Lemon Juice (76 g) [2 - 3 Lemons depending on how juicy they are.]
- ✓ Zest from Two Lemons

Let's Get Baking

1 Follow all directions for the Muffin Base recipe

2 Squeeze the lemons, careful to remove the seeds. You need 1/3 cup Fresh Lemon Juice. Zest the two lemons.

3 Once you have mixed all the dry ingredients and Rice Milk, add the Lemon Juice and Lemon Zest into the batter. Fold it all together, the lemon will make your batter airier and fluffier. Don't overmix it, just get it evenly combined.

4 Follow all baking instructions for the Muffin Base.

Blueberry Muffins

Gluten-Free, Dairy-Free, Soy-Free, Nut-Free, Corn-Free

Prep Time: 16 min, Bake Time: 20 min

There's almost nothing better than a warm blueberry muffin made with fresh blueberries. Slap a little dairy-free spread on there and it's heaven.

Additional Ingredients

- ✓ 3/4 cup Fresh Blueberries

Let's Get Baking

1 Follow all directions for the Muffin Base recipe.

2 Once you have mixed all the dry ingredients and Rice Milk, add the Blueberries into the batter. Mix gently one last time so you don't crush the Blueberries. The Blueberries should be evenly distributed.

3 Follow all baking instructions for the Muffin Base.

Apple Cinnamon Muffins

Gluten-Free, Dairy-Free, Soy-Free, Nut-Free, Corn-Free

Prep Time: 17 min, Bake Time: 20 min

Yum! Spiced apple goodness in these muffins. These are perfect in the Fall when apples are in season.

Additional Ingredients

✓ 1 large Granny Smith Apple Chopped into 1/4" pieces (you can peel the apple or leave the skin on if you prefer)

✓ 1 tsp. Cinnamon (2 g)

Let's Get Baking

1 Follow all directions for the Muffin Base recipe.

2 Once you have mixed all the dry ingredients and Rice Milk, add the Apple and Cinnamon into the batter. Mix one last time until everything is fully combined and the Apples are evenly distributed.

3 Follow all baking instructions for the Muffin Base.

Chocolate Chip Muffins

Gluten-Free, Dairy-Free, Nut-Free, Corn-Free

Prep Time: 16 min, Bake Time: 20 min

Great for kids, Chocolate Chips Muffins are sometimes easier than cupcakes. A quick, easy dessert.

Additional Ingredients

✓ 1/2 cup Dairy-Free Dark Chocolate or Semi-Sweet Chips (75 g)

Let's Get Baking

1 Follow all directions for the Muffin Base recipe.

2 Once you have mixed all the dry ingredients and Rice Milk, add the Chocolate Chips into the batter. Mix one last time until everything is fully combined and the Chips are evenly distributed.

3 Follow all baking instructions for the Muffin Base.

Summer Strawberry Muffins

Gluten-Free, Dairy-Free, Soy-Free, Nut-Free, Corn-Free

I created this recipe in the early years of Crave and only sold it during strawberry season. A funny but somewhat embarrassing story was that these little flavor bombs turned out to be simply too moist to sell in stores. Because we used fresh, juicy strawberries that I picked up from the market right before we made the muffins each morning, they were literally leaking out the bottom of the boxes. Sometimes there is such a thing as 'too fresh'. Live and learn! I hope you enjoy their moist texture in the comfort of your home instead.

Summer Strawberry Muffin Recipe

Gluten-Free, Dairy-Free, Soy-Free, Nut-Free, Corn-Free

Prep Time: 18 min, Bake Time: 22 min

Makes: 747 g, Enough for 12 Muffins

Tools

- ✓ Mixer or Beaters
- ✓ Whip Attachment
- ✓ Dry Measuring Cups
- ✓ Measuring Spoons
- ✓ Paring Knife
- ✓ Cutting Board
- ✓ Three Bowls
- ✓ Rubber Spatula
- ✓ Whisk
- ✓ Blender or Food Processor
- ✓ Muffin Pans
- ✓ Muffin Papers or Gluten Free Baking Spray
- ✓ Scale if you have one (for measuring by weight)

Ingredients

- ✓ 1 1/3 cup Lightly Pureed Fresh Strawberries (316 g) or about 2/3 lb.
- ✓ 1/2 cup Sugar (105 g)
- ✓ 1 cup Brown Rice Flour (150 g)
- ✓ 1 Tbsp. Baking powder (8 g)
- ✓ 1/4 tsp. Salt (1.3 g)
- ✓ 2 Eggs (99 g)
- ✓ 1/4 cup Palm Shortening (62 g)
- ✓ 1 1/2 tsp. Vanilla (6 g)

Let's Get Baking

1 Preheat oven to 350 degrees.

2 Destem the Strawberries, puree in a blender or food processor briefly, about 15 seconds. Don't puree them too long, you still want strawberry chunks. Combine the chunky puree with half the Sugar in a large bowl. Let sit.

3 Measure dry ingredients into another large mixing bowl- Brown Rice Flour, Baking Powder and Salt. Whisk out lumps.

4 Add Eggs to mixer. Beat on high speed with whip attachment until very fluffy. Add the other half of the Sugar.

5 Add Shortening and Strawberry puree to mixer and combine on low speed. Slowly add dry ingredients, half at a time. Beat on medium speed until fully combined. Scrape the bowl with rubber spatula, add the Vanilla and give one final mix to fully combine.

6 Spray your muffin pans or use muffin papers.

7 Fill each muffin cup or paper nearly full with batter (62 g). This makes about 12 muffins.
   Tip: Since these muffins don't rise much, feel free to use more batter if you prefer bigger muffins.

8 Bake for 10 minutes, rotate and bake another 12 minutes or until tester comes out clean. Muffins will still look moist but edges will start to pull away from the pan.

9 Let cool and remove from pan.

Autumn Pumpkin Muffins

Gluten-Free, Dairy-Free, Nut-Free, Corn-Free

This recipe for Pumpkin Muffins was first aired during my appearance on San Francisco's View from the Bay in the Fall of 2006 and was a huge hit with the hosts! I've updated the recipe to be even better than the original. These muffins are just the right amount of sweet and spicy and I love the airy, smooth texture. These are great for breakfast on those cool Autumn mornings!

Autumn Pumpkin Muffin Recipe

Gluten-Free, Dairy-Free, Nut-Free, Corn-Free

Prep Time: 20 min, Bake Time: 20 min

Makes: 867 g, Enough for 15 Muffins

Note: This recipe is Corn-Free as long as your Apple Sauce has no high fructose corn syrup.

Tools

- ✓ Mixer or Beaters
- ✓ Whip Attachment
- ✓ Two Bowls
- ✓ Rubber Spatula
- ✓ Whisk
- ✓ Dry Measuring Cups
- ✓ Measuring Spoons
- ✓ Muffin Pans
- ✓ Muffin Papers or Gluten Free Baking Spray
- ✓ Scale if you have one (for measuring by weight)

Ingredients

- ✓ 1/2 cup + 1 ½ tsp. Sweet Rice Flour (95 g)
- ✓ 1/2 cup Potato Starch (82 g)
- ✓ 2 ½ Tbsp. Tapioca Flour (17 g)
- ✓ 1 tsp. Cinnamon (2.3 g)
- ✓ 1 tsp. Allspice (2 g)
- ✓ 1 tsp. Baking Powder (2.7 g)
- ✓ 1/2 tsp. Baking Soda (2.7 g)
- ✓ 1/4 tsp. Salt (1.3 g)
- ✓ 1/4 tsp. Xanthan Gum (.5 g)
- ✓ 2 Eggs (99 g)
- ✓ 2 Tbsp. Soy Milk (28 g) [We recommend Original flavor. Vanilla changes the taste of the batter. Another non-dairy beverage of your choice is fine too.]
- ✓ 1/2 cup Sugar (100 g)
- ✓ 1/2 cup Brown Sugar, lightly packed (68 g)
- ✓ 1/2 cup Shortening (113 g)
- ✓ 1/3 cup Applesauce (87 g)
- ✓ 2/3 cup Pumpkin (166 g) [this is almost ½ of 15 oz. Canned Pumpkin]

Let's Get Baking

1 Preheat oven to 350 degrees.

2 Combine all dry ingredients in bowl and whisk out lumps - Sweet Rice Flour, Potato Starch, Tapioca Flour, Cinnamon, Allspice, Baking Powder, Baking Soda, Salt, Xanthan Gum. Set aside.
   Tip: If you can't tolerate soy, feel free to substitute your favorite original flavor, dairy-free milk alternative.

3 Beat Eggs and Soy Milk together in mixer thoroughly, use whip attachment on high. When very fluffy, after about 3 minutes, add both Sugars half at a time and combine fully on medium high speed. Then add Shortening until fully combined on medium high speed. Beat in Pumpkin and Applesauce.

4 Slowly add in dry ingredients 1/3 at a time. Scrape bowl with rubber spatula and give the mixture one final mix on high until completely combined.
   Tip: The pumpkin batter can also be used to make quick bread if you prefer a loaf shape instead. Simply extend the bake time, checking frequently to ensure you don't dry out the bread. Tester should come out clean, a few clinging crumbs are OK.

5 Spray your muffin pans or use muffin papers.

6 Fill each muffin cup or paper 2/3 full with batter (or 57 g). This makes about 15 muffins. Bake 10 minutes, rotate and bake another 10 minutes or until tester comes out clean. A few clinging crumbs are OK.

7 Let cool and remove from pan.

Variations on Pumpkin Muffins

Almond Pumpkin Muffins

Gluten-Free, Dairy-Free, Corn-Free

Prep Time: 23 min, Bake Time: 20 min

The toasted almonds give a little crunch and extra flavor.

Additional Ingredients

   ✓ 1/2 cup Sliced Almonds (55 g)

Let's Get Baking

1 Toast sliced Almonds in the oven or toaster for 2 – 3 minutes, just until you can start to smell them. Be careful because these thinly sliced pieces can burn fast!

2 Follow all directions for the Autumn Pumpkin Muffins. After everything is combined, add the toasted Almonds to the batter and mix until evenly distributed.

3 Follow all baking instructions for the Autumn Pumpkin Muffins.

Tip: For a little decorative flare, you can add some additional untoasted almond slices to the top of the muffins towards the end of bake time. The batter should still be wet enough for these almonds to stick to the top.

Walnut Pumpkin Muffins

Gluten-Free, Dairy-Free, Corn-Free

Prep Time: 23 min, Bake Time: 20 min

The walnuts give the Pumpkin Muffins a nutty, toasty flavor.

Additional Ingredients

✓ 1/2 cup Walnuts chopped into ¼" pieces (60 g)

Let's Get Baking

1 Toast walnut pieces in the oven or toaster for 2 – 3 minutes just until you can start to smell them.

2 Follow all directions for the Autumn Pumpkin Muffins. After everything is combined, add the Walnuts to the batter and mix until evenly distributed.

3 Follow all baking instructions for the Autumn Pumpkin Muffins.

Chocolate Chip Pumpkin Muffins

Gluten-Free, Dairy-Free, Corn-Free, Nut-Free

Prep Time: 21 min, Bake Time: 20 min

These are a crowd favorite. Pumpkin and Chocolate is an unexpectedly great combination.

Additional Ingredients

✓ 1/2 cup Dairy-Free, Semi-Sweet or Dark Chocolate Chips (75 g)

Let's Get Baking

1 Follow all directions for the Autumn Pumpkin Muffins. After everything is combined, add the Chocolate Chips to the batter and mix until evenly distributed.

2 Follow all baking instructions for the Autumn Pumpkin Muffins.

Cranberry Pumpkin Muffins

Gluten-Free, Dairy-Free, Corn-Free, Nut-Free

Prep Time: 21 min, Bake Time: 20 min

The addition of Cranberries makes these muffins a fruity, fall combo.

Note: This recipe is Corn-Free as long as you use dried Cranberries without high fructose corn syrup.

Additional Ingredients

✓ 1/2 cup Cranberries (75 g)

Let's Get Baking

1 Follow all directions for the Autumn Pumpkin Muffins. After everything is combined, add the Cranberries to the batter.
   Tip: Break apart any clumps of cranberries sticking together before you add them to the batter. This will ensure they will be distributed evenly when mixed.

2 Follow all baking instructions for the Autumn Pumpkin Muffins.

Chocolate Muffins

Gluten-Free, Dairy-Free, Nut-Free

Well, they may not be super healthy muffins, but wow are these good! Think portable, chocolate, hand-sized cake. These are double-chocolate with the chips as an added decadence. If you don't have the time to make cupcakes, these muffins can satisfy that cupcake dessert craving.

Chocolate Muffin Recipe

Gluten-Free, Dairy-Free, Nut-Free, Corn-Free

Prep Time: 20, Bake Time: 25 min

Makes: 1165 g, Enough for 18 Muffins

Note: This recipe is Corn-Free as long as your Applesauce has no high fructose corn syrup.

Tools

- ✓ Mixer or Beaters
- ✓ Whip Attachment
- ✓ Medium Pot
- ✓ Three Bowls
- ✓ Rubber Spatula
- ✓ Whisk
- ✓ Dry Measuring Cups
- ✓ Liquid Measuring Cup
- ✓ Measuring Spoons
- ✓ Muffins Pans
- ✓ Muffin Papers or Gluten Free Baking Spray
- ✓ Scale if you have one (for measuring by weight)

Ingredients

- ✓ 1/2 cup Unsweetened Baking Chocolate (85 g)
- ✓ 1/2 cup Palm Shortening (94 g)
- ✓ 1 cup + 1 Tbsp. Sugar (216 g)
- ✓ 2 Eggs (99 g)
- ✓ 1/2 cup Applesauce (130 g)
- ✓ 1/2 cup Sweet Rice Flour (79 g)
- ✓ 2 Tbsp. Tapioca Flour (14 g)
- ✓ 1/3 cup + 2 tsp. Potato Starch (68 g)
- ✓ 1/3 cup Cocoa (28 g)
- ✓ 1 tsp. Baking Soda (5.3 g)
- ✓ 1/2 tsp. Salt (2.5 g)
- ✓ 1 tsp. Baking Powder (2.7 g)
- ✓ 1/2 tsp. Xanthan Gum (1 g)
- ✓ 1 cup Water (227 g)
- ✓ 3/4 cup Dairy-Free Semi-Sweet or Dark Chocolate Chips (113 g)

Let's Get Baking

1 Preheat oven to 350 degrees.
Tip: If you have an oven thermometer, use it! Home ovens often aren't calibrated properly and can give you differing results each time.

2 Melt Unsweetened Chocolate and Shortening over a double boiler. While Chocolate and Shortening are melting, combine all dry ingredients in a medium bowl. Whisk to break up any lumps: Sweet Rice Flour, Tapioca Flour, Potato Starch, Cocoa, Baking Soda, Salt, Baking Powder, Xanthan Gum. Set aside.

3 Once the Chocolate and Shortening are runny, pour into the mixer. Add Sugar to the mixer. Using the whip attachment, mix on medium speed until sugar is completely melted.

4 Add Eggs, mix on medium just until combined. Then add Applesauce, mix on medium just until combined.

5 Scrape the bottom of the bowl with rubber spatula if needed and mix again until blended.

6 Add dry ingredients and water, half at a time and mix on low to reduce splashing. Give the bowl one final scrape and then mix on high for 20 seconds or so to fully combine.

7 Add the Chocolate Chips and mix on high for another 20 seconds to evenly distribute the chips.

8 Spray your muffin pans or use muffin papers.

9 Fill each muffin cup or paper nearly full with batter (or 84 g). This makes about 18 muffins.

10 Bake for 12 minutes. Rotate. Bake for another 13 minutes or until tester comes out clean.

11 Let cool and remove from pan.

Tip: This batter can be refrigerated for later use. It will separate but you can stir it up until it's blended again and use it the next day if necessary.

Spiced Banana Muffins

Gluten-Free, Dairy-Free, Nut-Free, Soy-Free, Corn-Free

One of my favorite things to bake growing up was banana bread. There was something so satisfying about mashing that over-ripe fruit and baking it into something so much tastier than it was on its own. That childhood nostalgia was the inspiration behind this recipe. The perfect way to use those bananas that are just ripe enough that you can't bring yourself to eat them!

Spiced Banana Muffin Recipe

Gluten-Free, Dairy-Free, Nut-Free, Soy-Free, Corn-Free

Prep Time: 25 min, Bake Time: 20 min

Makes: 691 g, Enough for 12 Muffins

Tools

- ✓ Mixer or Beaters
- ✓ Whip Attachment
- ✓ Three Bowls
- ✓ Rubber Spatula
- ✓ Whisk
- ✓ Dry Measuring Cups
- ✓ Measuring Spoons
- ✓ Muffin Pans
- ✓ Muffin Papers or Gluten Free Baking Spray
- ✓ Coffee Grinder if you need to grind Flax Seeds
- ✓ Scale if you have one (for measuring by weight)

Ingredients

- ✓ 1 cup = approximately 3 medium mashed, very ripe Bananas (250 g)
- ✓ 2 Tbsp. Rice Milk (31 g) [We recommend Original flavor. Vanilla changes the taste of the batter.]
- ✓ 1 ½ Tbsp. Tapioca Flour (11 g)
- ✓ 1/2 cup Sweet Rice Flour (79 g)
- ✓ 1/4 cup Potato Starch (51 g)
- ✓ 3/4 tsp. Baking Soda (4 g)
- ✓ 1 tsp. Baking Powder (2.7 g)
- ✓ 1/2 tsp. Cinnamon (2 g)
- ✓ 1/4 tsp. Salt (1.3 g)
- ✓ 1/2 Tbsp. Flax Meal (4g) [or if you prefer instead- 1/2 tsp. Xanthan Gum (1 g)]
- ✓ 1/3 cup Palm Shortening (77 g)
- ✓ 3/8 cup Sugar (79 g)
- ✓ 2 Eggs (99 g)
- ✓ Optional - Add 1/3 cup (50 g) of Dairy-Free Semi-Sweet or Dark Chocolate Chips

Let's Get Baking

1 Preheat oven to 350 degrees.

2   Mash your Bananas. Then mix with the Rice Milk and set aside.

3   If you choose to use Flax Meal instead of Xanthan Gum, grind Flax Seeds if necessary to make the Flax Meal.

4   Whisk together the dry ingredients to remove clumps and set aside- Tapioca Flour, Sweet Rice Four, Potato Starch, Baking Soda, Baking Powder, Cinnamon, Salt and Flax Meal OR Xanthan Gum.

5   Using the whip attachment of the mixer, cream together the Shortening and Sugar until light and fluffy, about 3 minutes.

6   Add the Eggs, one at a time, beating well after each to incorporate air. Add in the Bananas and Rice milk and mix on medium until combined. Add the dry ingredients, half at a time, mixing just until blended (this ensures a delicate crumb and prevents the batter from deflating). Scrape the bowl with the rubber spatula and give one final mix until fully combined.
    Tip: The banana batter can also be used to make quick bread if you prefer a loaf shape instead. Simply extend the bake time, checking frequently to ensure you don't dry out the bread.

7   Spray your muffin pans or use muffin papers.

8   Fill each muffin cup or paper nearly full with batter (or 57 g). This makes about 12 muffins. Bake for 10 minutes, rotate and bake for another 10 minutes. Remove from oven when tester comes out clean, a few clinging crumbs are OK.

9   Let cool and remove from pan.

Keep in Touch with Crave

www.cravebakery.com

cookbook@cravebakery.com

Crave less. Bake more.

Glossary

Bismarck Metal Tip

Decorating long, metal tips. Works best for filling DreamCups.

Blind Baking

The process of baking a pie, tart crust or other pastry without the filling. Pie weights are recommended when blind baking to prevent the crust from pulling away from the sides of the pan.

Crumb Layer

Your crumb layer is your initial, thin layer of frosting that can glue any crumbs down. Then when you add your second layer of frosting, there will be a clean finished look.

Double Boiler

A stove top apparatus used to melt chocolate without burning it, or cook any other thick liquid that would normally burn if not stirred constantly. It consists of an upper vessel containing the substance to be cooked that is situated above a pot of water. When brought to a LOW boil, the steam produced in the lower pot transfers heat to the upper pot.

DreamCups

DreamCups are a product we made starting in 2011. We had two flavors. Cherub DreamCups were vanilla cupcakes filled with vanilla cream. Tuxedo DreamCups were chocolate cupcakes filled with vanilla cream.

Fondant

Fondant (or rolled fondant) is commonly used to decorate wedding cakes. Rolled fondant is rolled out like a pie crust and used to cover the cake and create a smooth finish.

Frangipane

A European sweet and delicate almond filling.

Layer Cake

A layer cake is a cake consisting of multiple layers, usually held together by frosting or another type of filling. All of our cake recipes can be made into layer cakes. We prefer four layers of cake to create 4″ tall, fabulous looking cakes.

Pasteurized Eggs

Eggs that have been pasteurized in order to reduce the possibility of food-borne illness in dishes that are not cooked or lightly cooked. They may be sold as liquid egg products or pasteurized in the shell. Pasteurization is a process for destroying potentially harmful microorganisms in food by applying a precise amount of controlled heat for a specified period.

Pie Weights

Pie weights are typically small, somewhat heavy objects that are used to weigh down a pie or tart crust while it is being blind baked. They are used to prevent the crust from pulling away from the sides of the pan. Sometimes made from ceramic or steel.

Simple Syrup

A simple sugar and water mixture created by melting sugar in boiling water. In our cookbook, simple syrup is recommended to brush on cakes to replenish lost moisture.

Swiss Meringue Buttercream

Swiss Meringue Buttercream is prepared by cooking the egg whites and sugar together in a bowl placed on a pot of boiling water. The mixture is whisked while it cooks until the temperature of the mix reaches 140°F. The mixture is then removed from the heat and whipped at high speed until it forms stiff peaks and has cooled. The end result a beautiful, fluffy finish for your cake or cupcakes.

Index

37957445R00080

Made in the USA
San Bernardino, CA
28 August 2016